APPLY

MBA PROGRAM

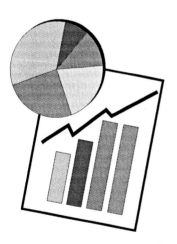

From Decision to Admission–

Interviews
with
Successful
Applicants

Lara Letteau, MBA

Bryan Goss

We would like to take this opportunity
to thank each of the individuals
interviewed and
all of the other people who
helped make this project happen.

Thank you

Bryan Goss and Lara Letteau

Author: Lara Letteau and Bryan Goss

Editors: Bryan Goss and Lara Letteau
Assistant Editors: Peter Goss and Loren Letteau
Cover Design: Beverly Goss

Applying to A Top MBA Program: From Decision to Admission
Interviews with Successful Applicants
By Lara Letteau and Bryan Goss

ISBN 0-9663944-3-7

Questions or Comments?
bgoss@md.nwu.edu

TABLE OF CONTENTS:

I. Introduction

II. Interviews

accepted into the accelerated four-quarter program at Kellogg School of Management for students with business backgrounds. He will be working for General Motors M&A division upon graduation.

Lillian Ho (page 51): Lillian is twenty-six years old. She graduated in electrical engineering from the University of Texas. Upon graduation, she went to work with McKinsey Consulting in Dallas. In 1997, she entered the MBA program at Stanford University where she was exposed to international finance and spent her internship in Singapore with a Venture Capital firm.

Patrick O'Neill (page 59): Patty is thirty-two years old. He attended the University of Notre Dame studying mechanical engineering before entering as an officer in the Navy. He worked throughout Europe, ending up as coordinator of a construction project in Naples, Italy. He left the Navy to start his MBA at Kellogg in Chicago. After working for a manufacturing firm in Chicago during his internship, he plans to pursue a career in the high-tech industry following graduation.

Cate Adler (page 65): Cate is twenty-seven years old. She studied civil engineering at Georgia Tech and then went on to work as a structural engineer in Atlanta. As she worked her way up to management positions, she recognized her interest in business and entered Harvard Business School. Her first summer was spent in a brand management internship at Coca-Cola.

Luanne Ellison (page 73): Luanne is forty years old. She graduated from Northwestern University in psychology and then went on to earn her law degree from Loyola. Luanne practiced law in Chicago, first working for US steel as a labor lawyer and then starting her own firm. Ready for a change after fifteen years of practicing law, she decided to go back to earn her MBA from Kellogg. At Kellogg, she majored in Health Services Management and wants to work in health care management in the future.

Maye Chen (page 81): Maye is twenty-seven years old. She was an economics major at Harvard before joining LEK as a management consultant. After several years in management consulting, she went back to business school at Wharton. She spent her internship at an investment bank in San Francisco and became exposed to different aspects of the high-tech industry - from venture capitalism to the basics of start-ups. Upon graduation, she will be forming her own start-up Internet company.

Daniel Grana (page 89): Dan is twenty-seven years old. He graduated from MIT in 1993 with a dual major in economics and political science. He then went to work for Merrill Lynch where he joined their Latin American group, spending several years in Mexico City. He matriculated at Kellogg in 1997 and spent his summer internship at Goldman Sachs in their equity sales. Upon graduation, he will be working at Putnam Investments, an asset management firm covering Latin America.

Cindy Lee (page 97): Cindy is twenty-six years old. She was born in Taiwan and grew up in Argentina before attending college at the University of California Berkeley where she majored in Communications and Spanish. Upon graduation, she worked for an advertising firm in Southern California before getting her MBA at Kellogg. She will be spending her summer internship at Procter and Gamble in Brand Management.

Michael Goodman (page 105): Michael is twenty-seven years old. He went to Duke University where he earned a BA in psychology. After undergrad, he joined LEK Consulting in Boston, focusing on strategy and Mergers & Acquisitions. He spent his third year with LEK on a project in Australia before returning the United States to start at Harvard Business School. He worked in brand management at Clorox for his summer internship.

Arti Finn (page 111): Arti is twenty-nine years old. She graduated from Kenyon College with a degree in English and Political Science. After graduation, she worked as a reporter for a magazine called India Today in Delhi. When she returned to the states, she worked as a political reporter in Washington, D.C and, later, as a corporate relations manager for an educational publishing company in New York. She entered Kellogg in 1997and spent her summer internship at Time-Warner's product development department. She will continue her work at Time-Warner after graduation.

Homero Gonzalez (page 119): Homero is twenty-seven years old. He grew up and obtained his engineering undergraduate degree in Monterrey, Mexico. After graduation he went to work for a subsidiary of a large cement company in Mexico. He spent four-and-a-half years in the departments of marketing and planning. He then applied to and was accepted to Kellogg Business School. He received a scholarship to attend from his employer in Mexico and will return to Mexico to work for the same company upon graduation.

Bryan Boches (page 125): Bryan is twenty-nine years old. He graduated from UC Santa Barbara majoring in Accounting and Economics. After graduation he practiced healthcare consulting in Canada and San Francisco before joining Morgan Stanley in Asia. He left Morgan Stanley to start at Wharton in 1997. Although he spent his summer internship working at Fidelity in their debt trading division, he will be helping to co-found an Internet start-up after graduation.

Sean Walters (page 131): Sean is thirty-one years old. He attended Williams College with a major in English. From there, he went to work at Monitor in their desktop publishing department. He started at Kellogg in 1998. He will be spending his summer internship in a special internship program set up to promote education and entrepreneurship. Through this program, he will be placed at Dynamic Trade Corporation working on e-commerce.

Erica Blewer (page 139): Erica is twenty-five. She studied business at the University of Texas at Austin. After graduation, she went to work at Pricewaterhouse Coopers, working as a consultant for bankruptcy and corporate restructuring. Her profession took her to Bangkok and Columbia for different projects. Her international experiences drove her to apply to schools with international programs. She ended up matriculating at Wharton in their special Joseph H. Lauder Institute program which provides a business degree with a special focus in international studies. She will be spending her summer internship working with Mercer Management Consulting in Latin America.

Henry Tung (page 147): Henry is 40 year old. He studied Human Biology at Stanford University before attending medical school at the University of California in San Diego. He then stayed in San Diego to complete his residency in anesthesia. Henry became very involved with different healthcare management ventures in the San Diego area before going back to get his MBA at Kellogg. Henry spent his summer internship working for McKinsey Consulting in their Orange County healthcare division. He will continue at McKinsey after graduation in their New Jersey pharmaceutical division.

Becca Hoffer (page 157): Becca is twenty-six years old. She grew up in Texas and attended the University of Texas in Austin where she majored in Finance. After graduation she went to work for Sanwa Bank in Dallas for a year-and-a-half. Subsequently, she worked for Pricewaterhouse doing Litigation and Bankruptcy Consulting. She then applied and was accepted to Harvard Business School under sponsorship from Pricewaterhouse. She spent her summer with Pricewaterhouse Coopers in their Human Resources division.

Sara Rudstein (page 175): Sara is twenty-eight years old. She attended the University of Pennsylvania earning degrees in Theater Arts and English. After graduation, she pursued her interests in theater management, first as a director/producer and later as a manager with the Shakespeare Theatre in Washington, D.C. After debating between pursing a Masters in Fine Arts versus a business degree, she decided to matriculate at Kellogg in 1998. She will be spending her summer internship honing her marketing and sales skills with Kraft in brand management.

INTRODUCTION

We decided to write this book after talking to classmates at the Northwestern Kellogg School of Management. We were extremely impressed with the diverse backgrounds of the students, as well as their differing paths prior to attending business school. Co-author Lara Letteau graduated from Kellogg in 1999. Co-author Bryan Goss, who audited Kellogg classes while in medical school at Northwestern, had previously written an interview-based book about the medical school application process and felt that a similar approach would be interesting and instructive to potential applicants to business school.

Instead of writing another "how-to" book, we attempted to complement, instead of compete, with them. For logistical details regarding applying to business school, there are a number of quality books on the market. For a complementary "up close and personal" viewpoint of the application process, keep reading. In addition to "just the facts," we believe that people want to hear personal accounts of the application process from top business school students. Personal friends attending business school are an excellent resource to obtain additional information about the schools. Similarly, in this book you will find nearly twenty detailed personal accounts, allowing the reader to say, "how does my background compare to this accepted student." Each student that was interviewed has a different story, a different background, and answers our questions in his or her own personal style. Therefore, from some interviews contained you will learn a significant amount about application essays. In other interviews, you will learn about detailed previous work experience. Each interview is unique and interesting for different reasons. It is our hope that the reader will identify with one or more individuals interviewed in this book. The information that the students share will help answer some of your questions and generate others. By reading about other people's experiences, you may think about your own, making your application and interviews easier.

This book gives a snapshot into the lives of successful applicants to some of the top business schools in the country. Students from Kellogg, Harvard, Wharton, and Stanford were selected to represent the supposed different school cultures of marketing, management, finance and high-tech entrepreneurism. As you will see, the students have opinions about the culture of each school and whether the public view is warranted. In this book, you will read first hand accounts from students of various backgrounds - including investment bankers, consultants, a small business owner, a military officer, a theater manager, a physician, an attorney and more. Prior to business school the students interviewed held positions in finance, marketing, consulting, human resources, nonprofit, health services management, and high tech within the above industries. After business school, many of the students have changed their intended career paths.

This book employs an interview format. This style allows each interviewee to expand on different meaningful and personal accounts from their application process. Each student interviewed answers questions encompassing his or her decision to go back to school, up and past acceptance and matriculation at a top business school. Some students then go on to talk about their summer internship and career plans following graduation.

The questions are approached in a consistent manner for each interview: The first questions pertain to the interviewee's background and previous work experience. The reader should be able to identify with one or more of the successful applicants and be able to relate to the factors or influences facing that person in the decision to go back to school. Additionally, students were asked to reflect on the benefits of a business degree in their respective field. Understanding their motivations will help you to answer that most important interview question - "Why business school?" You must be able to answer the "why" questions. We believe that these introspective questions to be most valuable. The answer may not be that you must have an MBA from a top school to advance to associate level at your company. Some students, as you shall read, chose an MBA to change career pathways.

Additionally, students were asked about sources of advisement. The students share information about whom they asked for advice and when and if they told their employer about applying to business school. Also, the students comment on where to find information about the different business schools. They offer some relatively easy ways to gather additional valuable information about the schools. Other questions pertain to the GMAT and how to best prepare. (Did they take a review course? How long did they study?) All of these questions are posed in the interviews with the answers depending on the interviewee's background. You can then compare your own background with what you read.

Students were then asked about the schools that they applied to, which ones and why. The answers to these questions allow the reader to learn about the personalities of the schools, and opinions to whether certain reputations are deserved. As you will read, many applicants just applied to the top schools, but others applied to schools with special strengths (international programs, etc). Most students interviewed say how many schools that they applied to and why. Many comment on the time constraints inherent in applying to a larger number of schools.

In the next set of questions, we ask the interviewee's about their actual business school applications. Students discuss the different essay questions and the image they tried to project. After reading something about the student's background, you can then see how and what they tried to emphasize on their application. Most try to project a unified image and you will be privy to how they chose to use their background to exemplify this image. Additionally, students interviewed comment on some of the specific styles and questions asked on the different school application. As you will see, some schools ask a battery of short answer questions where others ask only one or two extremely wide open multiple page essay questions.

Recommendations are required of each applicant to business school. These recommendations are important and can greatly influence acceptance or rejection from business school. Each interviewee discusses how he or she chose specific employers and professors. Should you choose someone with power and position or choose someone who knows you and has worked with you extensively? The insight gained from reading these interviews can aid the prospective applicant in the process of soliciting recommendation letters.

Also, although not required at each school, students discuss the different types of interviews, questions they encountered and how they prepared for them. As in any interview preparation, knowledge of what the applicant may face increases your confidence going in.

Additionally, most students interviewed discuss their involvement in extracurricular activities. What type of activities did they participate in and for how long? Although many of the students interviewed state that they were unable to participate in much outside of work, others did and expound on these experiences and how they added strength to their business school applications.

The light at the end of the tunnel is acceptance into a top business school. The interviewed students discuss their choice and why. Many of the interviewees have finished their second year and go on to discuss their summer internship as well as their future careers, reflecting on what they feel they gained from going back for an MBA.

Each of the interviews ends with closing thoughts and additional advice from each of the current business students. At this point in the interview, the students expand on previous answers or add other information that they deem important to the application process. Remember, each successful applicant is unique and has a different success story. Hopefully each reader can relate and reflect on the uniqueness of these applicant stories and thus be aided in his or her own application journey.

Applying to and enrolling in business school can be an enormous personal and financial investment -wrought with opportunity costs. The goal of this book is to give potential and current applicants additional information gleaned from the personal experiences of successful applicants to top business schools to make an informed decision about whether business school is the right choice for them. And, if business school is the right choice, the additional information gathered from this book will add to your ability to deal with the challenges of applying to a top business school.

INTERVIEW: HEATHER WELCH
Kellogg Graduate School of Management

Q: Can you tell me your age and your name?

A: My name is Heather Welch. I am twenty-nine.

Q: And can you tell me about your education prior to business school?

A: Sure. Freshman and sophomore years I was at Northwestern University studying economics and political science. I transferred to Stanford my junior year to do a quantitative economics program that Stanford had that involved a lot of econometrics and other not very fun things. But I at that time thought I might be interested in getting my PHD in Economics and considered going more the academic route. I did that program at Stanford and it was extremely challenging. I am glad that I did it now. It is the most difficult thing I have gone through academically. It was a lot of doing regression analysis without all of the nice programs that we have here at business school. We did a lot of programming, I guess, back then —writing every line for the regression to work. It was quite a challenge. I also spent time writing academic papers in a form that could be published.

Q: Did you continue your research activities?

A: I looked into working in economic research such as at a think tank, and I interviewed with a couple places in DC. One was the Moore International Economics Center and one was the Brookings Institute. And I was offered a position with them, but I decided that I really did not want to just sit at a desk and be all by myself working on one project and not interacting with other people.

Q: And also, during your undergraduate were you active in a lot of activities, business, or non-business?

A: Probably more non-business. When I was at Northwestern I was pretty involved with Special Olympics and there is an activities and organizations board there that I was involved with. I was also part of a sorority both at Northwestern and that transferred over to Stanford. I was the treasurer for the house at Stanford, so a little business. But I was not really in any more business organizations. I actually spent more time wanting to do things that were art-related in the first eighteen years of my life. I was going to be an artist. My mother is an artist, my father is an artist, and I was sort of on that track until I took a detour and went to Northwestern for a liberal arts degree. All of my work is in Des Moines, Iowa, and I didn't quite get it here.

Q: So what did you do in the working world prior to business school?

A: For the first year after school I worked in Chicago for a commercial bank, in their international trust area, global maturity services, as a financial analyst. I was helping to get out the monthly statements and make sure all the accounts were right for all the banks big pension accounts. They had the Illinois Teachers Association, American Airlines and other big accounts that had invested in international securities that we were in charge of monitoring. It didn't really challenge me. I began almost immediately trying to find something else and ended up back in California working for a financial advisory group, Deloitte and Touche, where I was doing evaluations of privately held companies in the high-tech, health care and a whole range of industries. It was a lot more challenging. It was a lot of industry analysis, a lot of company analysis, both qualitative and quantitative research. Doing financial modeling and meeting with clients and being part of the due diligence process, getting information and asking questions. It was much more service-oriented, and a lot more involvement with other people in my group as well as with the outside world. So I enjoyed that a lot. I transferred to their office in New Zealand for a year to help work on some projects down there.

Q: So, did you make your decision to go back to business school while you were in New Zealand?

A: I was at Deloitte and Touche for two years and then in New Zealand for a year, and then back in San Francisco for another year. I think when I first moved out to California and began working for Deloitte and Touche I realized that if I wanted to do something at all different, it was imperative that I have an MBA. Really seeing a couple managers that didn't have their MBA interview for different jobs, it was extremely difficult for them. I was also involved in our own recruiting process, sort of heading that up, so I was able to see what was out there and what people were doing. That made a huge difference and I wanted to pursue a different route and at that time I didn't really think that I wanted to be a valuation person for the rest of my life. I really enjoyed school; I really liked being in an academic environment. I always knew that I wanted to go back to some sort of graduate school and this seemed to be the best fit. I probably decided within a year of being at Deloitte and Touche that I wanted to do that. I was going to apply so that I would be at Deloitte for three years and then return to school, but when I was offered this opportunity to go to New Zealand I decided that it was an opportunity that I couldn't pass up. The partner wanted me to go for a year and then come back to San Francisco for a year so that I could still be a liaison between the New Zealand offices and our offices. They were trying to get the whole international financial advisory area more connected and they wanted to have that link until it was more established. So I agreed to do that and put off doing the application process for a year. After returning from New Zealand, I started sending for applications and thinking about what I was going to do.

Q: Did you tell your company that you were going to do this?

A: Yes. I really told them pretty early on that I wanted to return to school at some point. And they were extremely supportive. They were very supportive in general of continuing education. There is a charter program where you can become a certified financial analyst and I was involved in that - it's a three-year program with independent study culminating in an exam once a year. I was involved with that before and after I went to New Zealand. I hope to finish next year. They really encouraged their consultants who didn't have their MBA to get a CFA.

Q: So when did you take your GMAT?

A: I took it in 1996 when I was working with Deloitte and Touche right before I went to New Zealand - two years before I entered. I took it early because I actually initially thought about applying in '96, but decided to postpone when I was offered a position in New Zealand.

Q: Did you take any review courses?

A: No formal review courses. Several of my co-workers were taking it and I borrowed a lot of their materials and diligently went through all of their stuff and did practice exams. I studied for a couple months, mostly on the weekends.

Q: Would you study differently if you had to do it again?

A: I was pretty anxious about taking the GMAT. My grades are good, but I've never been the greatest test taker. I think I would have liked to take a course like Kaplan, but I didn't have the financial resources at the time and was extremely busy at work. I was happy with how I did on my own. Doing practice exams really helps.

Q: How did you pick the schools you applied to?

A: I applied to Kellogg, Stanford, and Harvard. I knew I was not going to be able to do six or seven applications and had seen co-workers struggle over a single application. I really knew I wanted to focus on two or three. I had a lot of people ask me why I didn't apply to the University of Chicago because it was so strong financially. But I knew that if I was going to be in Chicago, I wanted to be somewhere where I'd get a more rounded training. I knew finance was important, but I was immersed in this CFA program and doing financial work. I felt I would benefit more from a place with a stronger background in the areas I knew less about.

Q: Do you remember any specifics about your application that stick out in your mind? What image did you try to project?

A: Each school had very different formats. Harvard had eight very short essays - making you deliver the greatest amount of impact in only a few words. On the other hand, Stanford had two different questions of unlimited length. These were expected to be six to seven pages geared towards telling a whole story. One of the questions was- what events shaped who you are - very broad, open-ended questions. Kellogg's application were somewhere in between. All asked about what your plans are in life and why. I felt that Kellogg had the best spectrum of questions. One asked what one obstacle had you overcome which greatly impacted your life. Another asked if you were an admissions person interviewing yourself, what would you highlight about yourself. They also asked about how I worked in a team environment. Finally, they asked if there was anything else I wanted to tell the admissions committee about. I definitely wanted to let the schools know about all my experiences overseas and the importance of my family on my life.

Q: What other extracurricular activities did you participate in while you were working?

A: I spent three years working as a Girl Scout Leader in a low-income area. We would meet three times a month - it was a very big commitment. The girls were of all different ages. I started this with another woman that I worked with. I love working with children, and I knew that I wanted to do something educational. It was very important to me to feel that my work was making an impact. The girls were so excited about everything and had never been exposed to so much - we took many of them camping for the first time, carved pumpkins, went to museums, did art projects. It was amazing to see how much it affected them. I definitely miss having that aspect of my life. Also, I was also involved with an organization helping to fundraise for and raise interest in the San Francisco symphony. We tried to raise exposure to young adults by bringing the music into the schools.

Q: Can you tell me about your interview for business school?

A: Stanford did not have any interview and I did not have an interview with Harvard. The only interview I had was with Kellogg and that was done with an alumnus in San Francisco. The interviewer had graduated probably two or three years ago. It was pretty casual - more of a conversation while we went through my resume. Even though they definitely tell you that it doesn't matter whether your interview is on campus or with an alumnus, I felt that the ones on campus were definitely more structured. The people on campus probably know more of what their looking for, doing it day in and day out. I don't think it's necessarily advantageous to do it on campus, just that there is less variability in the types of interviews. On campus, you probably get more directed and tough questions. Some people prefer that instead of a more casual experience. On campus, you could also be interviewed by a current student and, from what I've heard, they can be the toughest interviews of all. I really don't think that it gives you a better chance of getting in if you interview on campus.

Q: Did you send anything in afterwards to update your application?

A: I did not. I was luckily able to get a good variety of recommendations early. Harvard required three recommendations, one being from a professor from undergrad, whereas Kellogg just required one recommendation and Stanford required a couple.

Q: Where did you get your recommendations?

A: One was from a senior manager at work. Another was a partner at work. Then there was the professor at Stanford. The people from work could, of course, comment on my work, but they don't know anything about my extracurriculars. So it was necessary to really fill them in on the other things that I was involved in. I felt that it should be from a more senior level person, which can be difficult since they tend to be so busy. It also is important to make sure that they write more than just a few lines. It's important that they get to know you and what you expect from their recommendation in terms of details. The more they write, the better.

I know students who had been placed on waitlists at school. In that situation, I think it definitely helps to ask the school what more you can do to supplement your application. They will often tell you if they would like to see another either personal or professional recommendation or an essay on a specific point in your application which wasn't emphasized in the interview. Be more proactive and try to demonstrate that you really want to be in this program. I have a friend who was placed on the waitlist. He flew to the school and personally talked with the admissions committee to find out what would make his application stronger. A lot of times they will directly tell you - your GMAT was a little low and maybe you should take that again. Or you need an extra year of work experience or more extracurricular activities.

Q: What did you did during you internship after your first year at Kellogg?

A: I was in New York City working with Goldman Sachs in their Equity Research Area. I was working directly with one of the senior research analysts who covered consumer products such as Procter and Gamble, Clorox, and Colgate. There were only nine summer interns there, each one of us working with a different analyst. Mine was the most quantitative, setting up and creating models to value different companies. I was responsible for writing the case reports and reconciling the conclusions for each company.

Q: Are you going to work for Goldman Sachs after you graduate?

A: Actually, no. I decided that I didn't want to live in New York City. I considered other equity research groups out in the West Coast, but decided to work for a boutique investment bank, doing merger and acquisition advising for high tech companies out in Palo Alto.

Q: Is there any other advice that you would give to someone similar to yourself when applying to business school.

A: Start early with the applications. The essays take so much time and thought. I probably spent every weekend for three months, doing a lot of revising. You should have them looked over for grammar and be sure that you've gotten across what you intended to. You don't want to be rushing it at the end. And if you don't get in this year and decide to reapply the following year, the schools will keep your old applications. So you want everything to be your absolute best effort because it will stick with you for a long time. The goes for GMAT as well. You don't want to just treat it as a practice exam to see how you do, because many schools will average all your results.

INTERVIEW: MARK PENDERGRAST
Kellogg Graduate School of Management

Q: Tell me your name and your age?

A: Marc Pendergrast and my age is 28.

Q: Briefly, can you tell me a little about your education prior to business school?

A: Graduated with a BA in History and Foreign Affairs from the University of Virginia.

Q: What type of activities did you participate in while you were in undergrad?

A: Two main activities that I was involved in: I was Co-President of the Virginia Ski Club, which was primarily a group that organized trips for students. We put on a spring break trip, weekly trips up to the local ski resorts, etc. I also was involved with the International Relations Club. That was a model U.N. club which had student debates on foreign policy issues at various college campuses throughout the year.

Q: After you graduated, where did you go to work?

A: I was very lucky to find a fantastic internship in Paris, France. I worked for a European affiliate of the American Software Trade Association. It was the European branch.

Q: What did you do for them?

A: I was a "Project Assistant," but that basically meant that I did everything. Everything from spread sheet reports on software piracy in Europe all the way down to delivering the mail. I was a "Jack of all trades."

Q: How long did you do that for?

A: One year. I was working there on a very temporary basis. I thought it was best to jump-start my career and get back to the U.S. This job exposed me to the world of high-tech and when I came back to the U.S., I found a job in the U.S. in the main office of the same trade association.

Q: Did you continue to work for them?

A: I worked there for another year and a half as a Research Analyst. I was the head research guy responsible for putting together monthly and quarterly reports on the software industry and running a data program that they had.

Q: And after that?

A: Then I sort of got sick of the public, non-profit world and decided to really jump into the high-tech industry. I was very lucky in that several people from my same trade association (which was based in D.C.) happened to have jumped ship earlier to go work for AOL, right outside of Washington. So I had plenty of contacts.

Q: What were you doing for them?

A: For AOL, I started as an Account Executive in their top 10 developments division. It was the so-called greenhouse area. We operated much like an ad agency in that we had many people that were providing us with information for our clients. Each client had a particular account executive that was responsible for handling the full gamut of issues. Everything from project management to getting resources to helping them learn the AOL system, marketing their product within AOL, doing market research, as well as how their products were doing on the service.

Q: Was AOL expanding like crazy when you were there?

A: It was booming like there was no tomorrow. It was very exciting. It was a good time to be at AOL. I had a very difficult decision to make at the end of my AOL career. Do I stick with the company?

Q: How did you make that decision to go back to business school?

A: I did it from a number of perspectives. Monetarily, I think that it would have been better for me to stay at AOL at least immediately, but I was thinking more long term. "Where did I want to be in 10 years?" I kept asking my self. What kind of skills or credentials would I need to be in that role? Eventually, I would like to run my own business. I have an entrepreneurial bug in me and I would like to know the nuts and bolts of how to run a startup. I am not quite sure what kind of startup to do yet, but I want to be able to have those kinds of skills and tools should I want to do it. Working at AOL was a great intro to the world of the online high-tech industry. It was fantastic exposure, but it did not provide me a wide range of skills. So I wanted to gain a wide range of skills so that I could diversify.

Q: So what was your decision based on?

A: It was based on career goals.

Q: Did you tell your company that you were interested in your MBA?

A: They knew all along. They were supportive. I was also lucky to have my direct supervisor, who happened to be a Kellogg grad himself. He wrote a fantastic recommendation for me. He gave me the whole scoop on what it was like at Kellogg and he really pushed the school for me. He was a huge support. In many ways, I could not have done it without him. I was honest with him from the get go. He knew I was interested in doing business school. AOL also saw the need for me and they knew what my ambitions were and they all agreed that this was something that I needed to do.

Q: When did you take the GMAT?

A: I believe it was Spring of 1997.

Q: Did you take any review courses?

A: Yes I did, I took the Princeton review course.

Q: How was that?

A: Very instructive. It really helped out. I am not much of a test taker. I don't do well on standardized tests. Some people don't have to study. I studied and still did o.k., but I certainly wasn't on the upper edge. I felt that I had to take a course like Princeton review. It really helped me.

Q: Did you remember how long you studied for it, how many months?

A: The course itself was 3 months.

Q: Do you feel it adequately prepared you?

A: Yes, I don't know how I would have done without it. What it really did was that it provided discipline for me because I was working at the same time and had a lot of things going on outside of work. It would have been very difficult for me to actually sit down and do it on a regular basis. If you are distracted by things going on or if you are not a complete motivator on your own, it is good to have a course like that to set the structure.

Q: Tell me a little bit about your applications? What schools did you apply to and how did you pick them?

A: I applied to Kellogg, Darden, and UCLA. I was considering applying to UNC as well, but I ended up not sending my application.

Q: How did you pick those schools?

A: A number of different criteria. I was looking for a school that had a broad perspective. I did not want a program that was too specific in marketing or in finance. I wanted a school that was well known for its general management focus. I think all four of those schools are known for their general management programs. I also wanted schools that I felt at home in. What I mean by that is that it had a good balance of school, recreation and in-school related activities (i.e. extracurricular activities).

Q: Tell me a little bit about the applications for those schools? What type of image did you try to project of yourself in the essays that they gave you?

A: I used a book that was very good at guiding me.

Q: What book was that?

A: It was Richard Montauk's book - How to Get into the Top MBA Programs. I highly recommend it. The central theme is to really craft a message around yourself. Almost like a puzzle. Your puzzle has to tell a story that fits together. Everything has to fit together. By that I mean, you have to have work experience, extracurricular activities, school activities as well as future goals and interests. All of those have to come together. My central message was that I was someone who had an international background with high-tech interests and who was very involved with extracurricular and community activities. It was a 3-D application. From my perspective, I wanted to set myself apart from a typical MBA applicant and, having done a lot of research on who MBA applicants were, I quickly realized that I certainly am not typical. At least when I was applying in 1997, there were very few people coming from high-tech. There were only a few people who actually left high-tech to go into MBA programs. There were plenty of Americans with an international experience, but I think I had a particular strong international application. My story fit together because I had worked in high-tech in Europe for a year and I had regular contact with friends and colleagues in Europe.

Q: You talked about one of your recommenders being a Kellogg graduate. How did you pick the different people to give you your recommendations?

A: I had a couple of people write recommendations for me actually. One of them was my direct supervisor at AOL. He was a Kellogg grad. I picked him primarily because he knew my work and he was also an MBA himself. So he could tell you what kind of skills and personality traits are important for an MBA program. I think his letter for Kellogg was the strongest. He could talk about the school itself and how it fit well with what I wanted to do. I also had him write out recommendations for the other schools for Darden and UCLA. I also had another supervisor, who I had worked with, write me a recommendation as well. Again, she knew my work as well. That was my criteria for picking the people to write my recommendations: those who had knowledge of and exposure to what I was capable of doing.

Q: During this process of applications, did you have any advisement? I guess you had some advisement from your superior at AOL. Did you have any other help?

A: I had help from some friends who were in MBA programs at that time. They provided quite a bit of guidance and also other colleagues at AOL that had MBA's as well. They helped me by reviewing essays and giving me pointers on what to push in particular essays.

Q: You said you were involved in some extracurricular activities? What were those?

A: After college, while I was living in DC, I was a rescue squad volunteer EMT. That was a great exposure for me. I think it was a fantastic experience. Not only did it push the leadership thing, but it also exposed me to an area of medicine that I thought was always interesting for me.

Q: How long did you do that for?

A: 2 years. The thing that I pointed out in my essays regarding the EMT is that is really showed a lot of commitment because it went above and beyond what most people are doing. It is something that I had to do on a weekly basis. Every week I had a duty night at the rescue squad for 2 years. Sometimes I would have 2 or three nights a week. It was a lot of commitment. You had to pretty much base your vacations and plan your social activities around it. This was stuff I did in addition to work. Totally volunteer. I would stay up to 2:00 or 3:00 a.m. running calls and then show up at work at 7:00 a.m.

Q: That took up a lot of time. Did you have other activities that you participated in?

A: Yes, I helped put together a couple of volunteer teams within AOL to participate in community projects. It was a serve-a-thon project. I organized a 60 - 70 person AOL team 2 days in a row. We essentially donated our time during a whole day. That was good from a leadership and coordination perspective.

Q: I know you probably had an interview at Kellogg. Did you have other interviews?

A: Yes, I had an interview at UNC and Darden. I had an UCLA's alumni interview. It was an AOL alum actually.

Q: Would you recommend trying to visit the school for the interviews or did you feel like the alumni interview is sufficient?

A: The alumni are great in terms of meeting people, but I think the whole point of going to school is that you are exposed to the whole environment there. I think that is an important criterion in choosing the schools. Do you feel at home in the environment? You can be exposed to a totally different side that you would not see from the school bulletin. For example, I had no idea that UCLA was such a modern campus and how focused it was on technology. I was very impressed with their facility. I don't think

I would have gotten that same kind of real feel had I not gone there. People there seemed incredibly friendly.

Q: So you feel that it is important to go to the school if possible?

A: I would not recommend applying if you had not already been to the school.

Q: What do you remember about your interviews?

A: I think the standard question I always got was why Kellogg or why Darden? They always wanted to know specifically what about me made me a good fit with the school. That was important because they expected you to have done some research about the schools and know about the particular activities and programs within the school.

Q: How did you prepare for your interviews?

A: I think a lot of research had to be done, reading through the Business Week reviews of business school, talking with people from those particular schools. I think it is key to talk with alumni and do research on the web site too. It was a big help. Schools are very forthcoming about criteria and student selection on the web site.

Q: Is there anything else from the interviews that you think is important to add?

A: I remember them being relatively low stress. I don't remember them being very confrontational or anything like that. I think all of the interviews were very laid back but I always felt that they were still watching me and evaluating me no matter what the situation was. In terms of advice for people during interviews, I would suggest that they pay particular attention to non-verbal actions.

Q: How so?

A: How you sit up in your chair, how you shake someone's hand, how you listen attentively while the interviewer is talking, and how you look the interviewer in the eye has a big impact. I think you have to be confident as well in your answers. People have to be somewhat comfortable with silence at least for a couple of seconds. I mean people should not immediately feel the need to shoot out an answer right away. It's o.k. to take a second to think about a question that they ask.

Q: Did you update your application after your interviews? Did you send any additional information?

A: I actually did the interviews relatively early in the whole process. For instance, with Kellogg, I came out and interviewed in October of 1997. I didn't send my application actually in until the following February or March. I had a relatively early interview with UCLA as well. I actually sent my applications in all after the interviews.

Q: Did you do that on purpose?

A: I think I just wanted to get the interviews out of the way because I realized that those took a lot of time to coordinate, especially if you are going out of state and out of the city. I wouldn't really have time while I was writing my essays. I would say it was on purpose.

Q: What did you do for your summer internship after your first year of business school?

A: I worked as a Product Manager at Intuit in their Quicken.com business out in California, again in high-tech. It was an MBA level position focused on market research and strategy consulting internally. I also did typical marketing promotions as well.

Q: Do you have any additional advice you would like to give somebody with a similar background applying to business school?

A: Two things. First off, start the process early. Don't wait until the last minute. I think what made my candidacy relatively weaker than it otherwise would have been was that I sent my applications in the last round. I think that was a mistake. The last round is when I would say a good half of the applications show up. Since most schools look at candidates by round, you want to get your application in during the first or second round. The second round would be the best. You need to plan well in advance. By planning, I would say 2 - 3 years out. I had a feeling after I graduated from UVA undergrad that I wanted to do an MBA. When I came back to Washington in 1993, I was already thinking about what kinds of things I needed to get involved with to prepare an application. That was a good 4 - 5 years before I even started applying. If you are going to be involved in extracurriculars, if you are going to be a leader within your company, you really need to think about these things. If you pull together things randomly at the last minute, it is not going to look coordinated. It is not going to look like you have a message or story to tell. My second piece of advice is for people on waitlist not to give up hope because I was on the waitlist at Kellogg. If you get a notice saying that you are on the waitlist don't assume that you are not going to get in. Do everything you can to make sure that they know that you are very interested in the school.

Q: How can you show them that you are interested?

A: A couple of ways. I had my recommender write another letter. Again, that really helped out. Second of all, I made sure to call them on a weekly basis asking them where I stood.

Q: Whom would you call?

A: I would call one of the admissions counselors.

Q: Were they accessible?

A: Sometimes, sometimes not. I got through one day to the Dean of Admissions. It seemed to have helped. You have to show that you committed to the school. You need to write another letter. I wrote another letter myself affirming what I had done since the last interview and application and again making sure that they know why you are a good fit.

Q: Now after you graduate where will go to work?

A: I am going out to Amazon.com. Hopefully to promote books like yours. I will be a Product Manager there.

INTERVIEW: KATIE PROCTER
Stanford Business School

Q: Could you tell me your name and your age?

A: I am Katie Procter and am 28 years old.

Q: Tell me about your education prior to business school?

A: I went to Philips Exeter for boarding school and Dartmouth College for undergrad.

Q: What did you major in college?

A: I was a government major.

Q: Did you have some extracurricular activities during college?

A: Probably the biggest one was varsity squash. Other than that, I had a bunch of other little things, like editor of an international magazine and sorority stuff.

Q: After your graduated, where did you go to work?

A: I went to work for J.P. Morgan in their Latin American Mergers and Acquisitions group. I spent four years in the M&A group. For two years, I worked out of New York on Latin American projects. Then I worked for one and a half years in Sao Paulo, Brazil and 6 months in Mexico City. In my fifth year, I switched over to the Latin American Equity Capital Markets. Basically, I was helping take Latin American companies public on the New York Stock Exchange.

Q: Are your fluent in Spanish?

A: I am actually fluent in Portuguese.

Q: Had you had language before you went down there to work?

A: I was pretty good at speaking Spanish. I actually learned Portuguese when I got down to Brazil. J.P. Morgan gave me Portuguese lessons in the mornings before work. So that is how I picked it up.

Q: So, it sounds like things were going great. How did you make the decision to go back to business school?

A: I think part of it was that I was a little burned out. I think part of it was also the desire to get a broader picture of what else was out there. Banking was pretty intense and I enjoyed it and learned a lot. But it didn't give me the time to just sit back and reflect and look at a lot of other career opportunities and see what else was out there. I thought I would stay in finance, but I wanted to see some of the buy-side opportunities like private equities, venture capital, and assessment management.

Q: What did you expect to get out of business school?

A: I wanted to get a much more balanced lifestyle. I wanted a broad exposure to a wider range of career choices so that I could decide where I wanted to go after that. Also, I wanted a great network of people with exposure to the technology and entrepreneurial fields which Stanford is known for, as opposed to what I had seen — which was the Wall Street banker, lawyer, and consultant type job world.

Q: When did you take the GMAT and did you take any review courses?

A: I took the Princeton Review. I took the course September 1996 and I took the GMAT in November, so probably 1 year in before applying to school.

Q: Was that hard to do with your schedule of bouncing back and forth to Latin America?

A: It was a little bit tricky. Luckily, they did have weekend courses, so I was able to take a Sunday course and study on plane trips. I would go through the book exercises that they gave me during the week. It certainly was not impossible. They do give you practice exams and exercises. It is an intense period.

Q: What schools did you apply to and why?

A: I applied to Insead in France. That was the most the international school. It has a one-year program in Fontainebleau. That was interesting to me in terms of wanting to learn to become an international manager and expanding my experience beyond just Latin America and the U.S. I also looked at Harvard, which was the most tradition place that people from J.P. Morgan went and then applied to Stanford.

Q: Stanford, mostly because of the entrepreneurial element to their culture?

A: Yes, the entrepreneurial element, the high technology focus, and a desire to get a little bit away from the New England Ivy League thing that I had grown up with. It was an alternative to that.

Q: Tell me a little bit about your applications. You obviously had plenty to write about, so how did you choose what you wanted to emphasize? What did you want to try to tell these people about yourself?

A: The applications were structured pretty differently, so that dictated some of it. The Harvard and Insead essays were very structured, very specific questions, with type, page format, and length specified. They really focused on leadership, career experience, and your key personality traits. You want to make yourself look good, but you also really wanted to represent yourself accurately. So, there were a lot of answers to certain questions (like who was your best mentor, what are your 3 personality traits) where I was just writing and re-writing my answer to make it sound as eloquent and polished as possible. Those essays were relatively straightforward for me. I chose to emphasize the areas in which I was different, so I did write about my Latin American focus.

I tried to show an ability to take risks because I think that is important in business. I think everybody shows leadership capabilities in terms of professional roles, extracurricular, etc.

The Stanford essay was actually much more free flowing. It basically asked, what where the biggest influences in your life. In addressing that question, again I had to go with topics that I felt very comfortable with. I wrote one about the influence of having 3 older sisters, and another about my experience in Brazil working as a volunteer with an organization there that worked with homeless children. I would say with the Stanford essay, I really wanted to accentuate what was different about me as opposed to emphasizing the more traditional aspects of my background. I don't think Stanford views itself as a traditional school. That is part of the reason for a very free flowing application form. They want to let you do whatever you want with it. For me the Stanford application was the hardest. Having specific questions and answering them is very easy for me. Coming up with whatever I wanted to write about is a little bit tougher.

Q: Whom did you pick to write your letters of recommendation?

A: At banks they have a definite hierarchy of analysts, associates, VP, and Managing Director. I think a lot of times at banks or consulting firms the focus is getting letters from the highest ranking people that you can. I though that was the wrong approach, because I wanted people to write about me that knew me very well. Otherwise, I thought they would write a very standard, boilerplate, distant type of recommendation. I chose three people all at VP level, one of whom I had worked with very closely in Brazil. I had worked with the second guy extensively on a management buyout project in Mexico. A third guy, I had worked with on US M&A deals. Each person was highlighting a different aspect of my career in a different location. Each of them had worked with me at a different stage in my career. I thought it represented me well in terms of sequence in my career, location in my career and some of the different tasks I was doing in my career as well.

Q: What position did you leave?

A: I left as an Associate. Actually, I could have stayed on and became VP without going back to business school. At that point, J.P. Morgan was not requiring people to go back to get their MBA.

Q: Did you have any advisement during your application to Business School?

A: One of my best advisors was my older sister who had gone to Columbia. She had started off in finance and switched over to brand management. She was incredibly helpful. I had a couple friends from J.P. Morgan who at the time had gone on to Harvard, along with a high school friend that was at Harvard. On the Insead side, I had a family friend that had gone to Insead so he really helped me out a lot with the process.

Q: You told me briefly about working with homeless children in Brazil. Can you talk a little more about the extracurriculars you were able to participate in before business school?

A: I had more free time when I was down in Brazil where my extracurricular activities were volunteer work at the homeless shelter, traveling around Brazil as well as taking Portuguese lessons.   When I was in Mexico City, I was taking Spanish lessons. I guess language would be a very big extracurricular focus for me. I also tried to take advantage of business trips in order to see some of the local countries. In terms of being able to fit in a squash or tennis game or jogging, I did that whenever I could. I would say in terms of extracurricular life before business school, I was somewhat restricted based upon my schedule. My hours had been in excess of 90 hours a week.

Q: Can you tell me about your interviews for school?

A: Stanford did not require an interview. I went to the Harvard interview and I had an interview with Insead.

Q: Did you go to the schools or did you do an alumni interview?

A: Actually, I went to Harvard. I did alumni interviews in New York for Insead. I did actually go and visit Insead on a weekend that they had for potential admits. I had seen the school. The interviews with Insead grads were pretty straight forward in terms of direct questions such as tell me about your background or your leadership. No real curve balls. They made a point of making sure that they talk about Insead and why it was different, the advantages of the one year program, and that it was a truly international program. At Harvard, they actually spent more time asking kind of random questions such as what are your dreams or how do you want to try to change the world... Less standard stuff. They chose to ask questions that were not on the application. I did not see a ton of overlap. There was more overlap of the questions on the Insead application and interview.

Q: Did you do any preparation for these interviews or did you just go in and let them happen?

A: I made sure I knew really well what I had written in my application. For instance, in a job interview you can make yourself look foolish if you don't know what you had written on your resume. You would look foolish if you went to one of these interviews and you are not well prepared on what you had said on your application. You don't want to present contradictions to them. I basically re-read my applications to make sure I was pretty knowledgeable about those. I didn't actually do any practice rounds with friends. Where I could, I tried to call people in advance, friends of mine, who had gone through the process and asked them what type of questions to expect.

Q: After all this, did you send any additional information besides the thank you notes?

A: No. I did not.

Q: What did you do for an internship after your first year of business school?

A: I worked at a T. Rowe Price Associates last summer in investment management and I was basically helping their portfolio managers pick stocks in the healthcare information technology sector.

Q: What are you going to do now after graduation?

A: I am actually going back to T. Rowe Price to work in their London office covering European and Japanese pharmaceuticals. I am still staying in the healthcare franchise.

Q: Any other advise you would like to give to somebody coming from a similar background as yourself who is applying to business school?

A: In terms of people that are coming from a similar background such as investment banking or consulting, I felt that Stanford was a really good choice as far as covering the traditional business school fields as well as a great exposure to entrepreneurial and high-tech areas. In terms of the recommendations, I think it is more important to get people that know you well and that can write you a very distinct recommendation than getting the highest level professional in the organization to write it for you. I think people sometimes forget that. You really have to be yourself in the applications. If you put a spin on yourself that isn't quite accurate, I think it appears that way—not quite genuine. I would encourage giving your essays to as many people as possible to get their feedback on them. So you can have an idea of how the admissions reader would perceive them.

INTERVIEW: KEVIN HADLOCK
Kellogg Graduate School of Management

Q: Tell me your name and your age.

A: Kevin Hadlock. I am twenty-six.

Q: And tell me briefly about your education prior to business school.

A: Sure. I attended Brigham Young University. My undergraduate major was business administration with an emphasis in international finance.

Q: And what other activities did you participate in during school, either business and non-business?

A: During school, most of the things that I did related to the student government. While I was at BYU, I was the associate vice-president of finance and resources for the student government and had responsibility for all of the student budget, as well as sitting on the committee that approved all the expenditures. So, it was very business-related. And I think the real benefit of these experiences was having a large amount of responsibility. It spent about twenty-five hours a week on these activities, so it was a pretty large commitment. On top of that I also had a business on the side where I did freelance financial consulting. And so whatever time was left in the week I spent with small business owners trying to attack a variety of different problems, albeit specific strategic problems or accounting system problems.

Q: So you were extremely busy. And were you married at the time?

A: I was married the last year of my undergraduate education.

Q: So, you also had a lot of responsibility. After you graduated, where did you go on to work?

A: I took a job with Morgan Stanley in investment banking. I worked there for two years. Most of the things that I did were analytical in nature — working on specific transactions and such; it was very intense as well. And that was in New York City.

The specific area was credit, but that's a little misleading. We worked on the M&A teams, we worked on specific debt collection, and gave advice on debt ratings and those types of things. So, it was just a variety of different projects, but it was tailored more towards the debt side. Another piece of the responsibility was doing annual reviews of all of our trading counterparts, so if Coca Cola wants to come in and trade equity options we would look at their credit and give them a trading line. So, we were doing the analysis on individual companies on an annual basis in specific industries.

Q: And then after that?

A: Then I applied to business school and was accepted.

Q: And how did you make your decision to go back to school?

A: It was a very difficult decision because I knew my age was going to be a disadvantage. I am a little bit younger than most of the people who apply. My lack of post-undergraduate experience I knew was going to be a disadvantage. But, from my position, being married and, at that point having two children, I felt like I wanted to go as soon as possible because the opportunity cost of leaving a job would just increase as time went on.

I think the thing that really made the decision for me was Kellogg's accelerated one-year program. Because of my business undergraduate degree, I was able to apply for the one-year program, and that to me was incredibly appealing — to be able to condense it down and not have to go through a review of the things I had already learned in my undergraduate business degree. So, I was in a position with Morgan Stanley were it would be another year of the same thing, and I just felt that if I could get in to a one-year program at a younger age, then I should go.

Q: That makes sense. So when did you take your GMAT?

A: I took my GMAT while I was a senior at BYU. The reason I did that was because I was thinking about applying to a third or fourth tier school directly out of my undergraduate education, so just to leave my options open I took it at that point. And then the job with Morgan Stanley opened up and I decided that having the business experience was essential and critical to really getting the most out of my MBA.

Q: Going back to the GMAT, did you take any review courses?

A: I did and I would strongly recommend it. I think it is essential if you want to score well. The review course will not necessarily make you more intelligent, but will familiarize you with the test process, with the format, and the types of things they are going to be asking, so you can be focused. I recommend that you do a lot of practice tests and you get that in a review course.

Q: Which one did you take?

A: I took one offered through my school.

Q: And so how long did you study?

A: In hours, including the course which met about 10 times for two hours each, I would probably say I spent between fifty and sixty hours over about a two month period.

Q: Okay. And did you feel this adequately prepared you?

A: Sure. It raised my score by about one hundred and thirty points. It was incredibly helpful.

Q: What schools did you end up applying to and how did you pick them?

A: I applied to Dartmouth, Harvard, Stanford, and Northwestern. The reason I chose those was that my background was so heavily weighted in finance that I thought I should look at some schools that had strengths in other areas as well. So I automatically ruled out MIT, Wharton, Chicago, NYU, Columbia and some other schools because I felt that they were so heavily weighted towards finance that I didn't want to pigeon hole myself into one specific area. My long-term goals were more suited towards general management. And so those four schools that I mentioned really fit that bill and my top choice in that group was Kellogg because of the accelerated program.

Q: So, tell me about your applications. What did you try to emphasize?

A: Well, the things I tried to emphasize were things only I could write about, that nobody else out there had experienced. Its not like the person picking up my application could say, well I've heard this story about thirty other times on different applications. I wanted to tell a story that only I could tell. You know you'll have people who have patents on products, that have written a New York Times bestseller, and only they can write those, and so I looked for things that only I could tell about. And part of that was, for example, I did a two-year volunteer mission in Taiwan, in between my sophomore and junior year at BYU. There are only about three hundred people who can write about standing in the rice patties helping an old farmer plant his field to make sure that he gets it in so he can have food to eat for the next winter. There are those types of experiences that only I could tell that help the admissions committee understand my character and who I am and what interests me and drives me. I think the admissions committee is much less concerned with the results of what you did. For example, I don't think they are so worried about awards or that they are just looking for a list of things that you have accomplished. I think they are more looking for a track record of success in whatever arena you participate in. They are not looking for someone necessarily that was the valedictorian of their class, or scored a perfect score on the GMAT. Those things are important, but they are looking much deeper into the character of the individual, at what drives them, what makes them unique, and what they can bring to the school. And, so it is hard to say this is the package that you need to present to the school, because there is no one package. Everyone is unique, and they are looking for that uniqueness. It seems somewhat abstract, or at least it did to me, but once you go through the process you start realizing it. And once you've been accepted, you start realizing that these are the things that they really like and that there is not really one right answer.

Q: How did you pick the people to write your letters of recommendation and who were they?

A: There are a lot of opinions out there on whom to choose. For me, I chose the people that I worked the closest with that could really give a good assessment of who I am. I didn't go to the Managing Director of the department for his title. I went for a vice-president, who is about three levels of management below the head of the department because he knew me the best. So, that was one letter. Another letter I had written by a man who I had worked very closely with in his office, when I was in Taiwan on my mission. I felt like he saw me in an environment that was a little unique, he could compare me to all of my peers who were kind of the same age, the same situation, and he could really give a good assessment of who I am. And I had another person who was a little more senior in management at Morgan Stanley with whom I had worked closely on several occasions and who was a very, very good writer. And this is something that I don't know if anybody else has emphasized, but when you are choosing people to write your letters, there are a couple criteria that were helpful for me. One is to make sure they know you very, very well. Two is to make sure they like you because there is nothing worse than going to somebody who really doesn't care for you very much. They are not as motivated to write a good letter. And third, make sure that they are an excellent writer. It really helps your cause. They may really like you a lot, they may know you better than anyone else, but if they can't write well. You know that doesn't mean you shouldn't choose them, but you may want to make some suggestions on content. You might write down some of the important things that should be included in the letter and give this to them to start with. If you are going to choose someone who is not a really gifted writer, help them through the process a bit, or try to encourage them to have someone else help them with it.

Q: And in terms of advisement during the process of your applications, did you have much, or were you on your own?

A: I was pretty much on my own. Everybody has some advice to give you, but I think that it is hard to give really specific advice that is really going to change the way a person approaches this. The advice that I received is similar to the kind that I am giving, and at the time I didn't understand why people were being so abstract and now I do. The advice was be yourself, don't think there is a standard answer because there's not, and if you give an answer that you think is standard then you probably are not going to get in. You need to be unique and tell a really good, cohesive story that you think frames you well and explains who you are. But, I didn't really have a lot of advice through the process.

Q: Okay. Do you remember any of the specific questions on applications that you think really allowed you to tell your story?

A: One of my favorite applications was my Stanford application, even though I was not accepted to Stanford. I felt that their application really helped them understand the person that was applying. They basically asked, "Tell us about yourself, who influenced your life, what major things happened in your life that formed who you are" — just tell us your story. And, you know, for them, that is kind of a screening process in itself because they can tell a lot about your character as well as a lot about your accomplishments and motivations from the things that you choose. Things come out in essays of this type that they can really decide if they want to let this person into the program.

Probably the most critical question and probably one that people should think about for more than just a week or two is what they want to do after they get their MBA. If they are really struggling with that question then it is probably too early for them to apply. I spent around six or seven months, if not more, preparing my applications, and that was the most difficult question for me to answer. Frankly I probably applied too early, because I really struggled with that question. I didn't really know what I wanted out of my MBA. Since then it's become very clear, but if people struggle with that question, that story has to be extremely cohesive and one that is very unique. If the answer to that question doesn't come to mind, then you may have to take some more time thinking about it.

Q: During your time at Morgan Stanley, what extracurricular activities did you participate in?

A: Well, I did a lot of things while I was at Morgan Stanley, one of which was as an assistant scoutmaster to a scouting troop in the area. It was a lot of fun. I was very heavily involved in church activities. I think the third thing that made me a little unique, especially when you consider I was in investment banking, was training and running in a marathon. I think that kind of showed a lot of drive and motivation despite long investment banking hours.

Q: Which one did you run?

A: Down in St. George, Utah. But, I also started to learn to play the guitar and just a variety of things to keep my life a little bit more balanced. Also, I have a wife and two kids, so that obviously takes a lot of time.

Q: Tell me about your interviews.

A: I went on interviews at Dartmouth and Kellogg.

Q: Are there any specifics that you remember?

A: I think that the interview process is really a chance for them to see if the person "in person" matches what they are on paper. And it really gives you another chance to tell your story and package it in a way that you really can't do on paper. I feel like my strength is really in person and not necessarily on paper. And I honestly believe that if Kellogg did not have their interviews I probably would not have been accepted. Interviews give the school the ability to look at another aspect of an applicant.

I feel like people should really take some time to prepare for their interviews. Have a couple of mock interviews with individuals. You know there is enough literature to prepare you for the types of questions they'll ask, and they are going to be really similar to the types of questions that they'll ask on the application. They really want to get to the bottom of what makes you tick, what motivates you, what experiences you have had, and what kind of a person you are. I think that is really the kind of thing they are looking for. Some of those answers don't translate well on paper. The schools that do interviews, I think, have a huge advantage in selecting their class over the schools that do not.

Q: And after your interviews did you send additional information?

A: I did. I asked another person whom I had worked with and who had seen a lot of MBA's come and go, as well as written a lot of letters of recommendation to write me a letter. At that time, I was on the wait list. And I asked him to send a letter directly to the admissions committee as another angle on who I am and to explain some things that maybe would help them see me in a little bit better light. The advice I would give to anyone who is put on a waitlist is to be a pleasant pest. Keeps in contact with the school, send additional information, update them on anything that has changed, and do it in such a way that it is not offensive. Leave messages, send faxes, and send letters. I would recommend that people do not constantly leave messages for people on the admissions committee to call them back, because they have a lot going on. If you are on the waitlist, that time period is extremely busy for them. If you can imagine, they have several hundred people

48

on the waitlist and if they had several hundred people calling to talk to them, it could be overwhelming and they wouldn't have time to do anything else other than return phone calls. So be a pleasant pest and try to find non-intrusive ways of getting your message across.

Q: And are you a first or second year?

A: Well, in the four-quarter program, we start in the summer and then we are basically second years from the outset.

Q: So, you don't do an internship.

A: No.

Q: I guess my last question is if you had to give a synopsis of advice to someone similar to yourself what would it be?

A: I would say start thinking about this process very, very early. The best candidate for business school is someone who has thought about business school since they were in high school if not earlier and tried to think about what they want to do with their life and their career. Sometimes the best business school candidate is the applicant who hasn't thought what do I have to do to get into business school. It's more of the person who says what do I want to do in my life, what are my business goals, what are my career aspirations. And I think that is the type of person business schools want to admit. Someone who is not doing things just to get into business school, but someone who is generally interested in a path and a career that is kind of unique that will naturally lead to a business school degree.

It is very difficult the senior year of your undergraduate degree to say, oh, what do I want to do, where am I going to work, where am I going to get a job. It is something that you think about very early on. I think that all the aspects business schools are looking for are all very important. You can't let your grades slip, you have to do well on the GMAT, and you have to be very involved in a lot of different things, especially business related activities. Someone who is going to school in a small town college may need to come up with ways of being involved in the business community and not just think that being captain of the swim team is going to do it for you. You've got to be very involved.

Q: And where are you going to work after business school graduation?

A: I'll be working with General Motors in New York City in their treasury department doing M&A transactions, doing some trading activities with commodities and currencies, those types of things.

INTERVIEW: LILLIAN HO
Stanford Business School

Q: Tell me your name and your age.

A: I am Lillian Ho and am 26.

Q: Tell me a little bit about your education prior to business school.

A: Before business school, I went to the University of Texas in Austin and graduated with a degree in electrical engineering. My extracurricular activities were related to the Engineering Council. It was a great organization, like an honor society where there were great friends and opportunity in leadership, etc. It gave me a chance to know the faculty and administration, some of whom I had as references and mentors.

Q: Where did you go to work after finishing school?

A: I joined McKinsey Consulting in Dallas. The primary thing I learned from my education was that I was not that interested in engineering. I was there for just short of 2 years and I did a variety of client work and tried to get as broad exposure as possible. My first year, I worked for technology clients, then I spent some time on electric utilities and then the retail industry. McKinsey gave me good formal training in how to structure problems, communicate at work, and approach different issues. What was also helpful for me was to be around people who had been through business school and get their opinion on the business schools that they went to, what they liked about it, as well as see how it matched their personality and see where my personality fit in on the spectrum. Then I also got feedback from people as to where they thought I should go to school and if that was the kind of environment I wanted to be in. At McKinsey, the majority of consultants went on to business school. I was trying to learn what business school was all about from my co-workers.

Q: When did you take the GMAT?

A: I actually took the GMAT in fall of my last year in college. During the previous summer, I had some extra time so I started studying for the GMAT. Since I was still in the test taking mindset as I was still going to school and used to taking tests, I went ahead and got it over with because I knew I wanted to go to business school within the next 5 years. I took it early and I was really glad that I got it out of the way. I did well enough. I think that your score usually won't get you into a school but it can keep you out.

Q: Once you decided to apply, how did you choose the schools?

A: I basically ended up always thinking that I wanted to go to Stanford, just from what I heard about the people. First of all, I loved the people that I had worked with who were from Stanford and they had nothing but the greatest things to say about the school. Everything about it was very interesting to me. It would be great to be in California. The environment of the school was good, very collaborative, very team oriented. They have smaller classes and I liked the fact that they challenge you to take more risks in terms of the courses and classroom work that you do.

Q: What other schools did you apply to?

A: I actually did not apply to any other schools.

Q: So you were either going to stay at McKinsey or go to Stanford?

A: I was pretty set on leaving McKinsey and I was working with some partners to find a way to go to Asia. They were helping me out by just putting me in touch with the offices there. Also I was networking with some other people in case the other options did not work out. I got a lot of questions about only applying to Stanford, where people would ask are you just that confident. My thought process wasn't at all that I was too confident that I was going to get in. That is why I was working hard getting a fall back plan because it was likely that I was not going to get in. I did not know how I would react personally if I didn't get in to Stanford, and I probably could have gotten into Harvard or Wharton. They are all great schools, but I really wanted to go to Stanford, and I didn't know if I would actually have the guts to turn Wharton or Harvard down and re-try for Stanford.

Q: Your plan was then, if you didn't get in, to try again?

A: Yes, I was going to reapply again and, if I didn't get in again, then I would rethink applying to other schools. I felt that I was young enough and had a lot of time ahead of me. I thought that I would give it a good shot and really go after it. Because I was working consulting hours, and plus I didn't think I would go to another school if I got in, I only wanted to work on the one application.

Q: What type of image did you try to project on your application? Stanford is pretty free flowing application, isn't it?

A: Yes. One of things I did was let them know who I was. So I had to figure out how to share who I am and open up to them as thoroughly as I could. As far as the image I wanted to project, I just wanted to make sure that I introduced myself, my personality, my values, and then I looked at their web site to see what kind of information they gave out. I wanted to be able to tell them why I felt so strongly that Stanford was the right place for me. All of the values that I saw in the site were things that I really cared a lot about.

Q: Like what?

A: Everything, like diversity. I grew up in a small town where there was a lot of racial tension. As an Asian, I didn't fit in really anywhere and it was something that I never really understood and addressed until after I got out of college and I was appreciating my heritage and trying to learn more about it. Stanford really encouraged diversity and that was something that was interesting to me. I also loved the freedom that they give to the students. They have created an environment where grades don't really matter. They want their students to feel comfortable, learn new things and take risks. Their belief is that, if you are worried about grades and competing with your friends, teamwork will be undermined. You may also be less likely to take "risky" courses which aren't in your field of expertise. Also, there is something really intriguing about being in Silicon Valley.

Q: Did you find Stanford students to come from entrepreneurial backgrounds?

A: In our class, there were so many start-ups and entrepreneurial people. There is a good chunk of people (20 or 30%) who went to go work for high-tech startups or ones they have started themselves. There is a changing number all the time, but at least 20 companies started in my class. Several have already gotten funding. I think we have a great network. One of our classmates has taken a lot of effort to organize a group so that everyone who has started their own business can get together regularly and share their ideas, questions, and work together. So when one person goes through the pains of a start-up, not everyone has to experience those same problems over and over. The team effort still pours over after graduation.

Q: Do you think that the school fostered it or was it the type of people who applied?

A: I think the school fosters it in how they structure their classes and how almost every class has a team project involving a large number of people. It's also due to the people — there are a lot of students at the school who are not afraid to take risks. People here are firm believers in doing what they want to do and not worrying about what other people say. There is a friendship among all of us. We just want to see the others succeed.

Q: How did you pick your people to write your letters of recommendations?

A: I had one from my McKinsey manager that I had worked with for about 1 year. I also asked the dean of students of the college of engineering, with whom I had a lot of exposure and a great relationship. The third one was a women that was the head of an institute that tried to match entrepreneurs and companies with investors. I worked for her while she was putting together a venture capital fund. I actually did an internship with them the last year of school when I was working part-time and still going to school.

Q: So did you send in additional letters?

A: Yes, from people at work — managers all the way up to partners that I had worked with. By that time, I had gotten to work with partners who were graduates of Stanford. I think at times it helped. Then I heard from other people that it is helpful to have alumni write your recommendation letters connecting them to you and the school. Just from the school's perspective, I could understand it because these are people who understand the school and understand the culture and they can speak directly to whether you would fit in to that type of school.

Q: So as far as advisement, you used some of the people you were working with to acquaint you with the Stanford mentality and to get information about the school. Did you have any other way to get information about the school?

A: I relied on the anecdotal information that I had from students and graduates. I had non-Stanford people tell me that they thought I should go Stanford. Everyone told me to go to Stanford. All the schools are promoting teamwork, a great environment, etc. It was really hard for me to differentiate based on written material. So for me it was a better litmus test to understand it from the point of view of people who had spent time there.

Q: Did you speak to any current students?

A: Most of people were from work. Some of my friends that I had worked with before had started business school and so I went out and did a visit to Stanford. I got in touch with my friends who where in the business school program, went to one of their classes, met some of their classmates and I got more personal, almost like validation of my interest in Stanford as a business school.

Q: During your work time, did you have much time to do any additional extracurricular activities?

A: For the most part, no. I got involved with my church. That was pretty much the only regular thing that I would do. I would try to find programs such as community activities and internal training sessions inside of work to get involved in.

Q: Did Stanford do a formal interview on campus or did you just visit?

A: I did a visit. I don't think the administration actually does formal interviews.

Q: What did you do after your first year?

A: I went and did an internship in Singapore. Students organized a big study trip to Asia during Christmas of my first year. During this vacation, I spent 3 weeks in Asia visiting a lot of companies. And so I was able to go back and do an internship with a Venture Capital firm that I had met with over there. Timing could have been a little better - I arrived in the middle of the Asian Crisis when business was a little slow. I learned about the venture capital industry and about a different country and had the opportunity to try out something different.

Q: If you were to look at someone like yourself applying, is there any other advice you would give to them?

A: Yes, to not worry so much about gaming the system or trying to project the image that you think they want to see. Get to know the school and the students. Once you find a match between yourself and a school, you need to do some research about the school. Be sure to communicate that match in your essays on why you think you will fit in. I think the questions at Stanford are open-ended like that because they want to see the reaction that they get. Having said that, I feel like I'm surrounded by the most amazing people with the most amazing accomplishments. I feel very lucky to have this opportunity to go to that school. I think most people feel very lucky.

Q: Do you think business school was all it was marked up to be?

A: Business school will go down as one of the best things that I have every done in my life. The people and the experiences that I have had here are fantastic. I think that I've gone through a lot of personal growth with who I am and what I want to do. I learned a lot from the classes and projects and working with people. I would recommend it to everyone.

INTERVIEW: PATRICK O'NEILL
Kellogg Graduate School of Management

Q: Can you tell me your name and your age?

A: Patrick O'Neill, 32 years old.

Q: Tell me about your education prior to business school? Where did you go to undergrad?

A: I went to undergrad at the University of Notre Dame and received a BS in mechanical engineering.

Q: What else did you do while you were an undergrad? Did you participate in any extracurricular activities or were you pretty focused?

A: I was ROTC. I was on the rowing team and I was on the boxing intramurals.

Q: After you graduated, where did you go from there?

A: I went into the Navy. I found myself on an island in the middle of the Pacific called Guam doing construction with a part of the Navy called the Sea Breeze. I found myself in charge of 13 folks, the youngest of whom was 6 years my senior, doing design work and some planning of construction. I went back to California then for 7 months after training and preparation for follow-up construction project in Greece and Sicily. In Greece, we were working with 2 groups, one on mainland Greece and one Crete, hopping back and forth between the two — closing one base down and building another base up. It was a different sort of Navy experience than most military folks in that I was always on land.

Q: What was the total period that you were working?

A: I worked for 9 years in the Navy. That was my first job. Following that I moved to Northern California were I had a unit of about 45 - 50 folks. We did 5 or 6 bases in that area. We did construction with a couple of different projects going on at any given time. I was the guy in charge of the whole thing. It was a lot of fun. That was for about 2 1/2 years and then I got a call again saying that it was time for me to move, where did you want to go? I said anywhere in the world, just send me to language school. I went to Monterey, California for 6 months to learn Italian and then was off to Naples, Italy.

Q: More construction/engineering there?

A: Yes. More contracting and engineering at that point. We were building a base in Naples and using Italian contractors to do the work for us. I did that for a couple of years and then came to business school.

Q: Was your rank advancing as you went through this?

A: I had normal rank advancement with being made Lieutenant at the 4-year mark. Then I checked out before the next advancement.

Q: How did you finally make the decision to go back to business school and how did you think it would benefit you?

A: A friend of mine while I was in Naples got me hooked on Business Week and Harvard Business Review and I started reading those and that really peaked my interest until I got to the point where I realized I wanted to do something a little more exciting than what the Navy wanted me to do. I looked for a little more challenge and a little more fun. I applied to a couple of schools and I happened that I got into Kellogg.

Q: So you got interested. Did you decide to take the GMAT at that point?

A: Yes, I got a couple of the study books.

Q: What study books were those?

A: Princeton Review and those kind of books.

Q: How long did you study?

A: Probably over 2 months.

Q: Did you take the GMAT overseas?

A: Yes. The military has a program were they set it up and you can take it on base.

Q: How did you choose the schools that you were going to apply to and which ones?

A: I looked at the Business Week rankings and I picked a couple of the top 5. I applied to Harvard, Wharton and Kellogg.

Q: You have a different background as far as most applicants to business school. What did you try to project as your image onto your applications or your essays?

A: I remember talking about my experiences with people, experiences overseas and viewing things differently. Motorcycle riding overseas, skydiving, and scuba diving. I discussed my management challenges and my language skills. I did a lot of negotiations on contracts and it was all in Italian.

Q: How did you pick your people to write your letters of recommendation and who were they?

A: One was a boss and one was the head of the Navy firm that we were working with in the States.

Q: Did you know them very well or did you pick them for their position?

A: I knew them both well. I actually wrote the recommendation letters and sent them to them saying, "Here is the first draft." My boss just signed it and the other guy worked it up pretty well.

Q: Did you have any advisement or input from friends or peers during your application?

A: No. I didn't know anyone who had done it.

Q: As far as extracurricular activities during your stay in the military, did you belong to any other organizations?

A: The military gives you a lot of athletic opportunities and there are always sports going on such as basketball, softball, and volleyball.

Q: Any professional societies?

A: In California, I was able to participate in the Alumni Association for Notre Dame. I also did Big Brothers.

Q: Which schools did you interview at?

A: I somehow didn't interview with Kellogg. I don't know how that happened. I did interview at Wharton. The first interview in my entire life basically. I bombed it horribly and walked out and bought a couple of books on how to do an interview.

Q: Is that what you would recommend to someone who is going through the process? What type of preparation would you recommend?

A: Any preparation. I went in basically cold. I was completely unaware that was what I was supposed to do and realized as I walked out of the interview that it had just gone terribly. I had my job as I graduated undergrad through ROTC without any interview. It was just a whole new world.

Q: After your applications were complete, did you send additional information to update your application at all?

A: No

Q: What did you do for your internship last summer?

A: I got a job here in Chicago with a multi-national manufacturing firm downtown called FMC.

Q: What did you do with them?

A: Business development.

Q: What industry are you looking to go into after you graduate?

A: Right now I am looking at either venture capital in Europe or working in the Internet field here in the states.

Q: Do you have any additional advice for somebody applying to business school that you would like to pass on?

A: The earlier the better. I waited until the 9-year mark and I am finding that those additional years in the military aren't particularly beneficial when looking for a job. I think that the military background helps and is appealing to big corporations. So I'd recommend coming out of the military as early as possible.

INTERVIEW: CATE ADLER
Harvard Business School

Q: Can you tell me your name and your age?

A: Cate Adler and I am 27.

Q: Tell me a little bit about your education prior to business school?

A: I studied civil engineering at Georgia Tech and graduated in 1993.

Q: Beyond your major, what type of activities did you participate in?

A: I was involved predominately in student government. I was also involved with an organization called Executive Round Table. Faculty and students would come together to discuss certain issues over dinner. I was also involved in a volunteer tutoring organization. When I was at Georgia Tech there was a large housing project across the street. In the middle of the housing project there was an elementary school, and Georgia Tech had a tutoring program where Georgia Tech students would be matched up with children from the school and they would spend several hours a week helping them study and getting involved in mentoring.

Q: After you graduated, where did you go to work?

A: I worked for large engineering construction company headquartered in Atlanta. I worked there for 1 1/2 years and then I went to work for a company called Stone Webster which was headquartered in Boston.

Q: What did you do for the company?

A: I was a structural engineer. The company built manufacturing facilities and my role was in the building.

Q: How did you decide to go back to business school?

A: Often, when you are practicing engineering, it is technically intense position where you don't have a lot of exposure to the big picture but are focused on the details. As I progressed through my career and moved up to a project management role, I realized that I liked the business side better. I started investigating business schools and initially thought I would go at night while I still stayed working, getting my company to pay for the tuition. But as I started researching more about the business schools, I decided that I really wanted to go back full time.

Q: Had you taken the GMAT or did you have to go and take it?

A: No, I had to take it.

Q: Did you take any review courses?

A: I did not, but I did study. I bought the Kaplan book with old review questions in it and I also purchased some old tests from the agency. I would spend a couple of hours maybe twice a week going over particular examples for about six weeks before the exam. I would also try to sit down on either a Saturday or Sunday with a good chunk of time to do a practice exam to see what areas I had trouble with and then I practiced those areas the following week.

Q: How did you decide which schools you wanted to apply to?

A: To be honest, I had a secret wish that I never articulated to anybody that I would love to go to Harvard, but I didn't really think that I had a chance to get in. Once I got my GMAT scores back, I realized that I did have a shot. I had done a lot of reading about the schools before I took the GMAT, so I knew that I wanted a general management program. Both Kellogg and Wharton were on my initial list, but because Wharton is known for finance and Kellogg for marketing, I decided not to apply to either one. I really wanted to stay in the curriculum under general management. I applied to four schools.

Q: Which four schools?

A: Stanford, Harvard, University of Virginia, and Dartmouth (Tuck).

Q: Where did you read about these schools? You said you did a lot of research?

A: I did. I had a bunch of books. There was one book that was called the Insider's Guide to the Top 10 Business Schools. There was another book called The 10 Day MBA. It was a really good overview of the kind of things you study in business school. It covers all the topics. I decided on the 4 general management programs that interested me the most and I also picked them based on where I thought I had a shot of getting into. I thought I had really good odds on getting into Dartmouth, but that Harvard and Stanford were kind of a shot in the dark.

Q: So with your background, what did you try to project onto your applications? What sort of image did you try to sell to them?

A: I had had a lot of experience at work managing and leading people and that was really what I tried to describe clearly in my application. I actually had people reporting to me that I had to manage. I had a lot of typical management things and challenges that I had to overcome, so I talked a lot about those and about managing people in the projects.

Q: Where you targeting Harvard with that approach?

A: I guess I was because I filled out the Harvard application first because it had the most essays and covered the broadest range of questions. All the other applications had essay questions similar to those of Harvard's. So, by spending the time on the Harvard ones first, I was able to easily answer the other applications later.

Q: You were able to cut and paste?

A: Yes, they were pretty similar actually.

Q: Did you think it was important to send in your application at a certain time?

A: I applied first round for all schools, but I tend to be a very timely, eager person. I had taken the GMAT back in March so by the time August came, I started working on applications. They were due the beginning of November. Some of the ones I applied for were due in December.

Q: So you tried to get them in right at their due dates?

A: Yes. I also used that software program called Multi-Application. It is a $50.00 program that you can buy and it has all the applications in it and you just enter your information your information once, which really saves a huge amount of time.

Q: How did you pick the people that wrote your letters of recommendations?

A: That was probably the hardest thing that I did because I didn't really want people from my office to know that I was applying to school. I chose 2 people outside of work but I also thought that it was important to have somebody at work. For my 2 outside people- one was a faculty member from my undergraduate school with whom I had a particularly close relationship. At the time I was finishing up undergraduate, I was debating going to engineering graduate school and he was a career mentor for me - the kind of person that I discussed my options with. I had him write a recommendation for me and then I also asked another person with whom I had formerly worked who had left the company. I really respected his style of managing people. For the third recommendation, I felt that I needed to get one from someone in my office, which was the most challenging thing. I decided to ask the vice-president of my company because he and I had a good work relationship and he was removed from what I did on a day-to-day basis. I felt that he would keep my secret.

Q: Did you have any advisement during your application process from either peers or colleagues or students from the schools that you were applying to?

A: I did talk to a lot of people about the school. I had a lot of friends from Georgia Tech that were actually in the different programs. I did contact as many people as I could to find out information in general about the programs. I didn't really get as much advice on the applications themselves, although there was one book that actually helped me quite a bit called Marketing Yourself to the Top Ten Business Schools. That helped put me into the frame of mind for writing the applications.

Q: During your work experience, did you participate in any additional extracurricular activities, either business or non-business?

A: Yes, I was really active in a fund raising program for the Leukemia Society. They use marathon races to raise money for their charity. I raised about $5,000 for the organization. It was great. I really enjoyed that program. I knew a patient and the patient's parents were about my age and I just really hit it off with that family. I was also active in local park conservancy in Atlanta. It was a park in the middle of Atlanta that was in pretty bad state of disrepair about 10 years ago and this organization acted to revitalize the park. I did a lot of work when I was there and helped to get volunteers.

Q: Did you have interviews for your business schools?

A: Yes, with Dartmouth, Virginia and Harvard.

Q: Did you choose campus or alumni interviews?

A: I did an alumni interview with Dartmouth and Harvard and was on-campus with Virginia.

Q: Can you tell me a little bit about those?

A: I had the Dartmouth interview first which was in Atlanta in a local hotel and it was very unstructured — kind of a free flowing. There were some questions, but it really didn't feel like an interview. He did not take any notes. He asked questions about my prior work experience and my future plans and about what I wanted to do. It was scheduled to be 30 minutes, but went over to an hour. It was a nice interactive conversation. It was more to let me know a little bit more about the school. He wanted to get to know me and the person behind the things that I did. Then I interviewed with University of Virginia on campus. That was more structured and I was there with 15 or 20 other students who were interviewing that day. I interviewed with second year students. It was in a small room on campus and much more structured with a list of questions. Then there was time for me to ask questions. That one went well. I felt like I was able to share information about myself and get information about the school. My Harvard interview was off campus again down in Atlanta with an alumnus in a local hotel. That was a cross between a structured interview and non-structured interview. She definitely asked good questions but she wanted to ask mostly about my work experience and examples of different skills that I demonstrated or how I dealt with problems.

Q: Did you feel an advantage or disadvantage to interviewing with alumni rather than on-campus?

A: Talking with people after the fact, I think it is an advantage to interview off campus. Because the people who interview on campus are interviewing people all day long, to me it was just a more stressful and pressured environment. You are sitting in a waiting room with other people who are interviewing that day. The interviews are much more structured, which I personally don't like as much. I think for me it was better to be off campus.

Q: After your interviews, did you update your applications at all? Did you send extra information?

A: No, I did not. All of the interviews occurred right before the decision date. There wasn't really any time other than send thank you notes. The thought really didn't cross my mind to update my application.

Q: How did you decide which school to go to?

A: I visited all the campuses and I was really impressed by what I had heard about Harvard and the people at Harvard and I think there was a little part of me that had always dreamed of going to a place like Harvard. When I found out that I got in, I visited more for a reason not to go than for a reason to go. I felt that it would be a great opportunity going to Harvard as well as being in Boston. I felt it really was an amazing place.

Q: If your were to give advice to someone similar to yourself, maybe an engineer applying to one of the top business schools, do you have anything else you would like to add?

A: I think the main thing that is really important to do is to take a careful inventory of everything that you have done. I think a lot of times people tend to take for granted the things that they do and not think that there is anything special or significant about them. I think perhaps when the schools are reviewing your application, how you view situations and what you take away from them are a lot more important than the situation itself. You may not have a list of really impressive credentials or work experience in your past, but if you explain about the things that have happened to you in an impressive way that shows that you learned or thought about something, I think that is more important than actually what you do. I would encourage people to take a careful inventory and really think about each little thing that they have done.

Q: Given your background now, how do you think business school is going to benefit you?

A: I think that was another reason that I choose Harvard because Harvard takes a very qualitative approach to learning and we discuss everything — communication skills are developed. I had a real strong quantitative background especially given I was a structural engineer, but I never had a chance to develop my communication skills. The balance that I am getting going Harvard is a really good balance for me and its going to develop my communication skills, written and verbal, more than any other school would.

Q: After your first year, can you tell me briefly about your internship?

A: I took an internship as a brand manager at the Coca-Cola Company. I wanted to come to a big brand company because, only having twelve weeks, I wanted some structure in my internship. I wanted to work as much as I could. I think brand management is a really good starting block for becoming a general manager. I had requested a small brand. Coca-Cola has over 20 brands that they manage. I wanted a small brand because I wanted exposure to all the different areas of brand management. When you come to a company like Coca-Cola and get a larger brand, a lot of times you are assigned a very specific project in a very detailed area, and you don't get exposure to anything except for your project. It was important to me to have exposure to all the different things that go on day-to-day in the life of a brand manager. I have had a great opportunity to do that with Fruitopia, getting exposure to everything- from launching a new flavor, to naming a product, to advertising and learning about what the PR agencies do. We have quantitative studies in local markets to see what is driving our strengths. I had a great exposure to a lot of different things. They have a great training program. They view it as an investment and are hoping to do all their recruiting, eventually purely through their intern program.

INTERVIEW: LUANNE ELLISON
Kellogg Graduate School of Management

Q: Tell me your name and your age.

A: Luanne Ellison and I am forty.

Q: And tell me little bit about your education prior to business school.

A: I graduated from Northwestern, class of '78. I finished college in three years, so I was a year younger than most people. And then I went straight to law school.

Q: What did you major in undergrad?

A: Psychology.

Q: And you went straight to law school?

A: Yes. So when I started law school, I was twenty. I went to Loyola and finished my JD degree in '81. Which is the usual thing; law school is three years. I took the bar exam in 1981. I then went to work for a firm that I had worked at in the summers. I wanted to be a lawyer since I was sixteen, so I had been working at this firm during the summers, and they offered me a job. It was a small firm that did litigation and that was what I wanted to do. I had a lot of opportunity to actually do something of substance, whereas at a bigger firm, a lot of times you get buried in the library and it's years before you actually get to go to trial or set foot in a court room. I stayed with that firm until 1984. And at that point I wanted a change. I felt I wasn't going to advance much further there. It was such a small firm that there was really not much opportunity for the future.

So then I went to a firm that did primarily labor law and worked in their general practice arm. I stayed there for about maybe two years and I was bored to tears doing general practice. Then I got a job as in-house Council at U.S. Steel. It's now called USX, but at the time it was still called US Steel. And I was there from '86 to about '89 in their Chicago regional department. It was a great job, but in '89 they decided to close many of their regional law departments. Headquarters for U.S. Steel is and continues to be in Pittsburgh. So they decided to close the law department but, they were extremely fair and I was given the option of taking a job with them in Pittsburgh at Headquarters Law Department. Or if I stayed in Chicago, they were willing to give me all the business that they had in Chicago and I could go to whatever firm I wanted to go to, or set up my own firm. I didn't move to Pittsburgh. By that time I had gotten married and my husband was pretty well established already at his own firm; he's a lawyer too. And moving to Pittsburgh wasn't really an option for him. So I decided to stay here and after talking to a number of law firms of various sizes, I went to a medium size firm, and I was really fortunate because I was able to enter the firm as a full equity partner.

Q: Because you were bringing in so much to the business?

A: Yes because that's important in law. So I was at that firm from about '89 to '92 and in '92, I left that firm to start a firm with some of my colleagues. We decided to start our own firm in '92 but it was a very bad mix. Things just didn't work out well. A year and a half later, I left there and I started my own firm. I had my own firm from '92 to right before business school started. I had my firm, which consisted of a few associates that worked for me, a support staff, a secretarial staff, and a suite of offices, and so-forth. It was a whole operation.

Q: So your went from having your own firm to deciding to go back to business school. What made you decide to go back to school?

A: Well, actually I had thought about business school from the year I got out of law school, back in 1981. I took the GMAT in 1982 thinking I might want to go. And I didn't do anything about it at the time. I had been in school, but now I was making some money and enjoying what I was doing. I put it on the back burner, but in the back of my head I kept thinking, I'd like to do this some day.

When I was at U.S. Steel, I had hoped that at some point, I could talk to them about tuition reimbursement for me to go at night, through an evening program while I worked but, of course when they closed the office, obviously that wasn't an option. And it really was still something I wanted to do. But while practicing law there really isn't much time for that kind of pursuit, especially if you do litigation work because you really don't control your own schedule a lot of the time. So you can't really think about going to school at night and working full time at a legal practice and having clients and trying cases; it just doesn't mesh that well.

So I really did put it on the back burner. When I opened my own practice I thought that time is going by and I haven't done this and I probably should if I'm going to do it. So I looked into whether I could use my GMAT scores again which I couldn't, so I had to take the test over again

Q: So did you just walk in and take the GMAT, or did you review for it?

A: I took a review courses at Kaplan. It didn't really change my score at all from the practice one. Actually, I scored better than I did when I took it in 1982, but the test was different too. By that point, the whole test had been changed. They added an essay portion to the test and so, on the Kaplan practice exam, when I first took the practice exam, I scored something like 710. And then on the real GMAT, my score was something like 720. But it helped in one way because I hadn't taken a test since the bar exam in 1981, and so it was just good in terms of practice. And to keep me from being so nervous! So even though it didn't help that much on the actual answers of the test, it helped my mental state to feel prepared for it going in.

Q: And then how did you choose what schools you were going to apply to?

A: Well I knew I wasn't going to move away from Chicago. Luckily, Chicago has two of the best schools in the country, Kellogg, and University Of Chicago, and those were the only schools I applied to.

Q: Okay, and did you think about the different personalities of the schools? Those schools have quite different personalities.

A: Well I didn't think about that until I got accepted to both of them. I didn't think about that at all. Because you have to understand my mindset was, "I've been talking about doing this for years. I've been thinking about doing this for years. If I don't do it now they'll never take me because I'll really be too old, so I better apply now and if I get in I'll worry abut it then." I had my doubts as to whether I'd get in, so I didn't even really think about the personality issues, until I got in both schools.

Q: What type of image did you try to project to the schools in your applications?

A: An honest image. I really didn't do a packaging job or anything like that. Some of the things I emphasized to both schools were the fact that I'd started and owned my owned business. Also, that I had positions of increasing responsibility and the types of cases I've handled. And my interest in health services management was another thing I talked about.

Q: How did you develop that interest?

A: Well I had been doing some work for hospitals and doctors as part of my practice, and so that was part of my initial interest in it plus some medical issues in my family. A serious medical crisis in my family exposed me to the medical system in great degrees more so than I think most people are exposed. So it's sort of a combination of having been an attorney working for health care entities and also having seen the consumer side of things that really lead me to have an interest in trying to get into that field.

Q: Okay. And how did you pick the people to write your letters of recommendations?

A: Well since I hadn't had a boss as such since 1989, I explained that in my applications. I'd been a partner in a law firm since '89. As a partner you don't really have a boss, so I had clients for whom I was corporate council write letters of recommendation for me.

Q: Did you have any advisement while going through the application process to business school?

A: I had my husband read my applications over with a fresh eye and critique them. Other than that nobody else looked at them.

Q: During the time that you were running your own firm, were you involved in extra curricular activities, professional societies and things like that?

A: The vast majority of my activities I did outside work were law-related. I was a member of a committee of the Bar Association and I joined the Chicago Chamber Of Commerce. Also, I had some involvement with the Women's Business Development Center.

Q: Tell me about your interviews.

A: I was just trying to project myself pretty honestly. One impression that sticks with me, as being kind of funny, and I've told this story before but, at University Of Chicago, I was interviewed by a student who was obviously quite a bit younger than me. And when he looked at my GMAT scores, he said 'Boy, these scores are really good, especially for someone your age; at your age the brain turns to mush." Fortunately, I am very thick-skinned and it just runs right off my back. But I thought it was hilarious that this person that was interviewing me didn't realize how inappropriate it is to comment on somebody's age. So that stuck with me. At Kellogg, I was interviewed by an employee of the school, one of the admissions office personnel, so obviously that situation didn't come up. But basically I just tried to portray myself honestly and answer the questions they asked. And I let them know that even though I waited so long to apply it wasn't because of lack of interest or focus, it was just circumstances in my life that inhibited me from applying sooner.

Q: So you got into both schools. That was a nice situation to be in. How did you decide which school you wanted to go to?

A: Well I think in my head Kellogg had always been my number one choice because it had a dedicated health services management program and also because it didn't have the reputation for being quantitative like the University of Chicago. Of course, I had a certain loyalty to Northwestern having gone there for my undergraduate years as well. So I think even though I gave U of C some serious thought, I think Kellogg was always my number one choice between the two.

Q: When I got accepted at U of C, I got this phone call from the head of the admissions office. He called me up very excitedly and said that we want you to come and not only that but the people that read your application said we'd be crazy not to accept you, and that your application was the best one they read. He may say this to everybody, but he sounded genuine enough to really make me feel good.

For Northwestern, I got a phone call during the week before the final decisions were to be made from somebody in the office of Kellogg, asking me if I had applied for the evening program or the day program. And clearly my application was for the day program. They had no reason to have thought I'd applied for the evening program. Then they went on to ask what I planned to do with my business if I did get in, which I thought was irrelevant. When I did get in I didn't receive a warm and effusive phone call like U of C, I just got the letter saying congratulations, you got in. But that's what made me even give U of C the consideration. I did because they seem to want me so much more and that had an effect on me. But in the end, I decided that I'd go with Kellogg because that had really been where I wanted to go to begin with.

Q: Interesting. Given your background, how do you think your MBA is going to benefit you in the future?

A: Well, I don't know if it will. Let's say that for starters, and in the interest of full disclosure here, I'm not sure that it will benefit me in the future. It has benefited me now because I've learned a lot, and although I realize that business school is not a place that you go to learn for the sake of knowledge for me, in some ways that's what it's been.

Q: It's been a personal goal for so long?

A: Yes exactly, and I have learned a lot. And it has been a challenge and has stretched my mind in ways that it was not stretched. In different ways than it was stretched as a lawyer, so it's benefited me in that regard. From a career stand point I am not entirely sure. The jury is still out on that one. I don't really want to take an entry-level type position, and because of that I've ruled out a lot of things that may have been potential options. But I'm hoping at this point perhaps the best niche for me would be something that combines both my legal experience and training with what I've learned in business school. That would be ultimately the best situation that could happen for me.

Of course I realize those type of positions don't come along every day and when they do you really have to ferret them out. So as I say the jury's still out on those kinds of benefits to me. It may well be I'll end up back in a purely legal job but that's OK. This is something I wanted to do. For me I've considered it basically a sabbatical from practicing law. It's been both challenging and enjoyable for me.

Q: The last question I have is do you have any additional advice to someone like yourself, an attorney going back to business school?

A: Well, I would say that, if it's possible, don't wait as long as I did. Being older does present certain issues in terms of not just the job situation, but also the social situation. So that would be one bit of wisdom — don't wait as long as I did. If you have an opportunity and you have the desire, do it sooner and you can always pick up where you left off. It's only really 2 years. And then secondly, just from the standpoint of a lawyer talking to other lawyers I would say, it might not be a bad idea to combine the two. You know they do have the program to do that. Northwestern certainly does. And I think in terms of saving time it does that and you're kind of killing two birds with one stone. So that's one option that I think people should consider. If I had it to do it over I would probably do it that way. You know you end up with both degrees, it's a shorter period of time overall, and then you don't even have to worry about taking time out from your career to do it.

INTERVIEW: MAYE CHEN
Wharton School of Business

Q: Please tell me your name and your age?

A: My name is Maye Chen and I am 27.

Q: Can you tell me about your undergraduate education prior to business school?

A: I was an economics major at Harvard.

Q: What else did you participate in as an undergrad? Were you active in other extracurricular activities?

A: Yes. I guess my main activity was that I was on the crew team. I was a coxswain for the woman's crew team. I wasn't exactly a relaxing job but it was great. I think that was one of the things that helped get me a job and also get me into school. It's a perfect combination of teamwork, leadership and dedication.

Q: How many years did you participate in crew?

A: I did that for 3 years. I also did a couple of other things, but this was by far the most demanding. I got the most out of it as well.

Q: Where did you go to work after undergraduate?

A: LEK. It was called the LEK Partnership and then it became LEK consulting. I worked there for 4 years. I started as an associate and then, after your second year if you stayed and they liked you, you were promoted to an associate consultant, which is the step between being an associate and being in a MBA consultant position. After that I actually decided to stay a fourth year and I was promoted to consultant.

Q: What type of projects did you work on?

A: It was a very generalist program so we worked on all sorts of industries. I worked on cases on fire engines, amusement parks, biotechnology, and household cleaning products. I don't think I learned much in terms of individual industry expertise. However, I learned how to learn about an industry really quickly.

Q: After that, how did you then make your decision to go back to school?

A: Before coming to school, I spent another six months in Taiwan and I decided that I wanted to go back to school for many reasons. One reason was to take a break from work and to meet a whole bunch of different people. I felt that consulting had so much hands on experience that I really didn't expect to learn that much from the classes. Before I did that, I went to Taiwan for six months to learn Chinese and ended up actually finding a job there that led me into my current entrepreneurial interests. The job was with a well-established freight forwarding company. The founder's son and his friend, who had just graduated from Harvard Business School, decided that the two of them would try to turn around the company and take it public. That gave me a taste of entrepreneurial work as opposed to being an outside consultant. That experience led me away from wanting to work in a client service industry. It was a tough decision as to whether to go back to school or whether to stay with the company. At that point, I just wanted to get back to U.S. and look for a good business school.

Q: When did you take your GMAT and did you take any review courses?

A: I took the GMAT in 1994 while I was stilling working at LEK and I didn't take any classes but I did get one of the books at the bookstore and basically studied it for about an hour four times a week for about a month before the test. Also, I studied a little bit more on the weekends.

Q: Was that adequate for you?

A: Yes. It was fine.

Q: What schools did you apply to and how did you pick them?

A: I applied to Harvard, Stanford, Wharton and Berkeley. At the time, my goal was to be back in California. I didn't get into Stanford. I was waitlisted at Harvard. I got into Berkeley and Wharton and was seriously considering Berkeley. But when I got there I felt like the students seemed to emphasize the presence of Stanford and it made it seem like it was going to be an uphill battle job-hunting after business school even if I were out in CA. The whole point of being in California was to make my subsequent job search there easier. In the end, I decided that the Wharton network and name would be more valuable. I am not sure if that is really true or not. That was just the perception that I had after being there for a day or two.

Q: Tell me a little bit about your applications? What did you try to project of yourself in those applications?

A: Actually I felt like I had a really run-the-mill background. I was a solid candidate but not that unusual. I tried to get across more personality than anything else. I am a pretty straightforward person and I said things in my essays that I think other people might not of felt comfortable putting in. I wrote about a crew race and how another boat had crashed into us during warm-ups and one of the lines I said in the essay was about scaring the "shit" out of my rowers. I knew that it wasn't the most proper thing to say but that is how I felt about it and so I wrote it. I did things like that. It is really hard for me to say whether that worked or didn't. They might have said, despite that, we will let her in. I wouldn't really recommend it, but I felt like a lot of the process was being so careful about the image you were getting across and so I felt like I needed to be a little more real about it. For example, one of the essays talked about who your mentor was and what it was that you admired about him/her. I started by quoting a Kenny Rogers song. I just did silly stuff that was relevant but I tried to give it a little bit more personality.

Q: Who did you choose to write your letters of recommendations and how did you choose them?

A: I chose partners in my firm and also my boss at my Taiwan firm to write me the letters. I also actually got a LEK client to write me a letter. In retrospect I think it would have been better off sticking with the LEK people, because the client did not know me well enough to write things off the top of his head and so he ended up asking me for suggestions. If someone knows enough to write a letter themselves and not ask for any suggestions, I think you are better off. I basically asked partners that I had known for at least two years and they could tell stories. I think they were able to tell stories of me when I first started so it showed some progression. Then my boss in Taiwan, I had only worked for him for a couple months but we worked really closely together.

Q: Did you have anybody that helped or advised you during your application or were you on your own?

A: I did have a couple of friends look at it. I definitely leaned on one of my friends that was in business school and then my sister who had read my college applications. I did have people look at them and give me comments. Some of my friends who had five or six people read their essays told me that their essays became muddled. I sounded like their essays became more the combination of five different people's thoughts rather than their own. From what they told me, they thought they had lost a little focus.

Q: While you were working, were you involved in any extracurricular activities?

A: No, I wasn't. Because LEK is a small firm, you end up doing a lot of what they would call extracurriculars that are all firm-specific. I was on one of the committees that developed the professional development curriculum at LEK, which was the ongoing training for our employees. I did some English as a second language tutoring in the Boston Chinatown. That was actually through Harvard. It was one of those tough things where we were travelling, not as much as other consulting firms, but enough to the point that it was hard to get involved and really make a difference in an organization. I guess I was a little more transient because I spent time not only in Boston, but also in Manila, LA and Chicago.

Q: You weren't able to continue on a crew?

A: Crew is a special animal. It is like one of those things that is all encompassing. I actually did look into it a little bit, but decided not to do that.

Q: Tell me about your interviews.

A: I did my Wharton interview when I was in Taiwan. They actually had a representative come to Tokyo and Taipei and maybe one other spot and strangely enough he is now a first year at Wharton. It was an official Wharton representative doing an interview in a hotel room in Taipei. My Harvard interview was in the admissions office. I did not do any alumni interviews.

Q: Did you update your application at all or did you send any additional information?

A: No.

Q: So how did you decide between Berkeley and Wharton?

A: When I first looked at, it seemed like a really tough decision. It was a decision of almost complete opposites because Berkeley is so small and focused on things like non-profit and entrepreneurship, and Wharton was huge and had the reputation for being finance-oriented. It was California vs. Philadelphia. I was actually thinking the name wouldn't make much of a difference because I was planning to be in California anyway so I thought that the Berkeley name would be strong enough. I think it probably is. I just felt like going to Wharton would give me a lot more flexibility because it is more widely known and there are so many alumni. I think so much value comes from meeting people. There are a lot of benefits to being in a smaller program, but there are probably even more benefits to being part of a big program. You can still get the closeness of the small program. You still meet a lot of great people and make close friends; you still have the opportunity to be in smaller classes, but you have the option to go big when you want to. That was one of the things that really pulled me.

Q: Then the culture, did it turn out to be very finance-oriented?

A: No, I was really surprised. I braced myself to be around a lot of investment banker types. I really didn't feel that at all. There are definitely some people that fit that stereotype and that seemed very competitive. However, there are so many people that were so laid back and not competitive all. Competitive in the sense that they push themselves but not competitive with other people, which makes it a really great environment. I am sure that I would have been happy at Berkeley as well, but I have no regrets about coming here.

Q: What did you do for your internship after your first year of business school?

A: I went to San Francisco and I worked at Robertson Stevens, which is an investment bank, not because I wanted to be an investment banker. It fell at the intersection of a lot of different interests that I had. It was a small, high-tech focused investment bank. I was trying to decide between going into private equity or venture capital vs. going to a startup. I felt like this would be a great opportunity because they have all sort of ties to venture capital. They work with startups all the time and it was located in San Francisco and I had never lived there before, but I kept thinking that I wanted to so this was a good way to try it out.

Q: Now you are starting a company? What type of company are you starting?

A: Yes. An Internet company. It is basically a virtual dressing room. There are a couple of companies out there that are doing it right now. We think that we have a different approach. It is like an intermediate step between going to a shopping mall vs. shopping through a catalog. You can try on clothes on the web and see how it looks on you.

Q: Is there anything additional that you would like to add for someone who has a similar background that is applying to business school?

A: I would say take care of the easy stuff. The GMAT is so straightforward that I would say put the time in and do well on that because it makes your life easier. If there are any organizations outside of work that you are really interested in, try to make the effort to get involved. That is something that I wish that I had done. Not for the business school application process, but just as another experience to have done that you can bring to the table at school.

Also, find a mentor. From a business school application point of view, it's really helpful to have someone who knows you well and who can write a good recommendation. From a longer-term point of view it is so incredibly helpful. My mentors have help me make contacts in fields that interested me (private equity and venture capital, which are notoriously difficult to break into without connections), and they have given me all sorts of advice along the way. I found my mentors through work - managers and partners who I worked with on projects or simply whose desks were close to mine in the office.

INTERVIEW: DANIEL J. GRANA
Kellogg Graduate School of Management

Q: Tell me your name and age.

A: Daniel Grana and my age is 27.

Q: Tell me a little bit about your undergrad education?

A: I graduated from MIT in 1993 with a dual major in economics and political science. In terms of activities, I founded and was President of the Undergraduate Economics Association and outside of that I did basically a lot of sports.

Q: Where did you go to work after that?

A: I went to Merrill Lynch and was an investment banker for four years in their Latin American group. The first two years I was in New York and the last two years I was in Mexico City helping open the Mexico City office.

Q: Can you tell me what types of projects you were working on?

A: I was a financial advisor to companies and governments and I also helped to raise capital for companies and governments. I did both debt, equity and equity-linked products such as convertible bonds. Normally the M&A stuff is also excluded as a separate group, but because Latin America was such a unique market, we also did some M&A as well.

Q: How did you make your decision that you wanted to go back to business school?

A: I was thinking very hard about what I wanted to do "when I grew up." Obviously, the reason why I chose investment banking in the first place fresh out of college was that I didn't really know for sure what I wanted to do after college. I felt that the generalist position in investment banking where I could see a lot of different industries and look at their strategy would hopefully point me in the right direction. I used investment banking more as a springboard and the time had come finally to move on. I had decided that while investment banking was very exciting, it just was not what I wanted long term.

Q: Did your company know that you were applying to business school?

A: As part of the application for business school, 3 letters of recommendation must be done. Obviously, one or two of them should be from your current employer. I had to disclose my intentions to them both because I think it was the responsible thing to do and also because I was hoping to get very good letters of recommendations from the people I had worked for.

Q: Whom did you end up choosing for your letters of recommendations?

A: I chose both the head of the Latin American investment banking group in NY and I chose my informal mentor. She was the senior investment banker in Mexico City outside of the head of the group in Mexico.

Q: Did you choose them because you knew them well or did you choose them for their position?

A: I knew my mentor extremely well. I had worked extensively with her. She is a very tough investment banker but I learned a tremendous amount from her. Since I had done a lot of work for her, I knew that she would be able to give a very good letter of recommendation- one that points to actual things that I had done. I did not have as much contact with the other person who wrote a letter for me, but I felt that given I was basically the only analyst hired for his group in my year, he did know me. Also, he obviously knew that many of the investment bankers were asking for me to work on their projects. In a way I chose him for his position and that he knew of me.

Q: Going back to your GMAT. Did you take any review courses for that?

A: Yes, Merrill Lynch at the time basically paid for any of the review courses. I think they had an agreement with Kaplan. They paid for us, so that was sort of a fringe benefit of being an analyst.

Q: So they really encouraged people to pursue an MBA?

A: The program is essentially a two-year analyst position. They don't guarantee anything beyond that. So there is a lot of turnover after the second year. Many people try to go to business school, but generally two years is not enough any more. It used to be enough, but now business schools are looking for more. If you do really well, you get invited to be a third-year analyst. Then an even more select club would get invited to become an associate without an MBA, which was what I was given.

Q: You obviously did very well with your group.

A: I felt one more year in investment banking would really help my career or rather my learning experience so that I why I chose to stay another year beyond my third-year analyst position. A lot of my colleagues left.

Q: Let's talk a little bit more about the GMAT. You took the Kaplan course.

A: They had a special program for professionals that was Saturdays and Sundays, which for an investment banker was perfect because I had very long hours during the weekdays. I actually took this course in New York before I went to Mexico. It would not have been available to me in Mexico. I took the course, I think it was a 2 - 3 months process but it was every Saturday and some Sundays.

Q: Do you feel that it adequately prepared you?

A: I think it did a fabulous job. I highly recommended it. I probably would have scored 100 points less than I actually did.

Q: When it came down to choosing the schools that you applied to, how did you pick them, how many where there, and which ones did you choose?

A: The decision to choose business schools should not be taken lightly. You should do a fair amount of research. Basically, I looked at my background and I knew I had an extremely quantitative background and my economics degree was more math than economics. My four years in investment banking was very quantitative and so consequently I felt I shouldn't go to a quantitative school, but try to broaden my experiences. I ruled out the University of Chicago. I did apply to Wharton but I don't think I really seriously considered it because their name brand is also finance. I did not want to label myself in finance. I felt that I needed some marketing and organizational behavior, some of the softer skills. That is what directed me toward Kellogg, even though I applied to the other top 3 business schools — Stanford, Harvard, Wharton.

Q: Can you tell me about your applications? Obviously, your work was focused on finance, but it sounds like you were trying to open up your possibilities with business school. What type of image did you try to project in your applications?

A: I wanted to project somebody that was not just a typical investment banker. I did not want them to think that I was just another cooker-cutter investment banker applying to business school. I actually had some very unique international experiences, given the fact that I did not just do analyst work. Our group was severely understaffed so I ended up doing a lot of stuff that bankers 2, 3 or 5 years senior to me would only get to do. Also, I thought it was important to convey the significance of my Hispanic background and my whole father's side of the family leaving Cuba because of the Cuban Revolution and what impact that had on my life.

Q: Did you have any specific advisement during this time of application?

A: I guess I was a little isolated being in Mexico, so only my mentor, who went to Harvard was really giving me any insights. She was removed enough not to know what they were currently looking for.

Q: During this time, while you were in Mexico and South America, were you able to participate in additional extracurricular activities?

A: Basically, I suffered through a brutal 2 years in New York, where there were some weeks I worked 120 hours a week. After that, I realized what a brutal lifestyle investment banking was and so consequently I tried to work less in Mexico. I took advantage of the fact that I was in a foreign country and all my friends were locals and they took me around to weddings, restaurants, villages, and around Mexico. That was my extracurricular activity — learning about the culture. To me it was a time of decompressing after a very intense two years.

Q: Do you have any advice for the business school interviews?

A: It is very important to know the school and know what they are looking for. For example, Kellogg obviously is looking for people who can work in teams because a lot of our school class projects are in teams. Now obviously the particular interviewee would know that, so you just can't say that you are a teamwork kind of person. You actually have to back it up with examples. You have to sound sincere. You have to do your homework, you have to know what they are looking for but you also have to actually have done it. However strange that may sound.

Q: Anything else for other schools?

A: I interviewed for Wharton. They like international experience and so I spent a fair amount of time talking about that in my interview.

Q: How did you decide on which school to go to?

A: Again, given my background, I would have liked to have gone to Stanford just because I guess quality of life was important. I was leaning toward Stanford. Of the schools that I did get into, my first choice was Kellogg.

Q: Is there any blanket advice that we did not go over that you would like to give to somebody from your similar background?

A: Applying to business school is not something that is easy to do as an investment banker because you have to spend a fair amount of time on your applications. One piece of advice is to start early. Another is that you can't suddenly start doing the application and then decide at the last minute that you have to sound different or get on a particular type of project in order to be different. You have to look at the application one or two years in advance and try to see or learn about the schools. Try to see what you are missing. The third piece of advice, probably the most important, is you have to know what you are doing. You have to know why you are going to business school. You have to have a game plan. If you don't have a clear game plan in your application, saying you want to go to this school for these reasons, that it compliments your background, etc. If you don't say that or have a clear direction, then no one wants to take you. There are so many other people that do have clear directions and business schools want winners. People who have thought through what they want to do and connect A, B, C and D and go forward.

Q: What did you do for your internship after your first year of business school?

A: When I came to Kellogg, I changed directions dramatically. I have decided to stay in the financial industry but not as an investment banker. I wanted to do asset money management, basically working in a mutual fund, working on portfolios. Unfortunately, those kinds of jobs are extremely rare for the summer, so my next best thing was to work at Goldman Sachs in their equity sales and trading program. Given that I already had the quantitative background in investment banking, I did not need that. I saw a different side of the business. And that's what I did. Fortunately for me, after graduation I've managed to land a very good job at Putnam Investments, in an asset management fund covering Latin America.

Q: Given you background, do you feel like your MBA is giving you what you wanted?

A: Yes. I think that is has opened my eyes. Not only the classes, but also the other students. Actually I think you do most of your learning outside the classroom, not in the classroom. It has opened my eyes to certain things that as a financial person I would not have thought of. Obviously, given my career, even though I will be in the financial world, I will be picking stock so I have to pick winners and winning strategies. I really did need the marketing and the strategy I learned in business school.

INTERVIEW: CINDY LEE
Kellogg Graduate School of Management

Q: Okay, so can you tell me your name and your age?

A: Okay, my name is Cindy Lee and I'm 26 years old

Q: Tell me about your previous education prior to business school.

A: I went to UC Berkeley as an undergrad. I majored in Communications and Spanish. People were very surprised that I came to business school because they thought I had no quantitative skills.

Q: Obviously, you proved them wrong. What other kind of activities did you participate in beyond academic in your undergrad?

A: I was involved in the Chinese student union and I was in charge of doing the annual culture night stage show. Besides that, I worked a lot during undergrad. I did tutoring, I worked at the doctor's office, I worked at a super market, pretty much everything.

Q: So you helped pay for your undergrad education?

A: Yes. I didn't have a lot of time to devote to extracurricular activities because work. But I tried to get involved in honor societies and doing charitable events.

Q: As I understand you grew up internationally, is that correct?

A: Yes. I was born in Taiwan, and I grew up in Argentina. Actually my family moved to Argentina when I was nine. So I grew up there until I was seventeen until I graduated from high school. Then I came to the states, and went to Berkeley for my college education.

Q: So, where did you go to work after graduating from college?

A: After undergrad, I moved to Southern California and worked in advertising for four years. The advertising agency I worked for targeted the Asian American population. We helped corporations tap into to this ethnic segment.

Q: So you worked there until you went back to Kellogg for business school?

A: Yes, but I did move around within the company. I worked in the media department for a couple of years and then moved into account services where I had face-to-face contact with clients. So it was a well-rounded advertising experience.

Q: And during the time that you were working did you have time to participate in some other activities?

A: I was a member of some organizations like the Young Executive Program and the Asian Professional Exchange. Also, through my work, I got involved with a non-profit organization helping refugees. I helped out doing extra workshops on things like how to find a job and practical things like that.

Q: So how did you decide to go back to business school?

A: Actually when I graduated from Berkeley I was already looking into graduate school in journalism. I was accepted but then wasn't sure if that was what I wanted to do. So, I decided to take a year off to work and I liked my work. I liked advertising, so I stayed. I was still thinking about going back to school to get a master's degree in public relations. Then, I changed departments from Media to Account Services and I had a lot of client contact with Marketing Managers and Brand Managers. And I thought that's cool, I want to be a Brand Manager. I could have moved from advertising to the client side, but it would have taken more experience. With business school I could spend 2 years, and then just jump into the client side. I had that goal in mind. I wanted to get into marketing. I wanted to be a Brand Manager and in order to get there I needed an M.B.A.

Q: So after you decided that you wanted to go to business school, you had to take the GMAT. How did you study for the test?

A: Oh I procrastinated a lot. When I decided I wanted to do business school, I started thinking right away about the GMAT. The first thing I did was buy a book.

Q: Do you remember what book?

A: I think it was Barron's because I used them to study for the GRE. I started two years before the exam doing one test a month. And that wasn't really helping a lot. By the time I picked up a little I'd forget again. After two years I wasn't progressing much because I was kind of on and off. I ended up going to Kaplan to get myself motivated. I think Kaplan was more to pay the money and then push yourself to study. I didn't do the full course because I didn't have time. When you take these tests you need to know your strengths and you weaknesses. What I needed the most was to work on the verbal section. I thought I would do well on the quantitative section (because I usually did well) but I had to make sure and because that's where I get my scores. I think the best way to study is to take one or two months and just concentrate and do it.

Q: Can you tell me about the schools you applied to and how you picked them?

A: Well there were so many schools I wanted to apply to, but it came to a point that I had to narrow it down because I only had so much time left. So I narrowed it down to six schools: Kellogg, Anderson, Stanford, Berkeley, Wharton and Michigan. I had some motivation for staying on the West Coast. And then Michigan and Kellogg were good in marketing, and Wharton because it's one of the top Business Schools. I didn't apply to Harvard because I was more marketing-oriented. I eliminated some the schools that I felt were more finance oriented, like University Of Chicago and Columbia. I think they are really good schools, but I didn't apply because they were known as finance schools and very quantitative. And then I also eliminated schools based on geographic reasons like University of Virginia and Tuck. It really helped to narrow it down to six schools. I know people who applied to ten schools, but I couldn't afford the time. I wanted to concentrate and put a lot of time into each application.

Q: And how much time did you spend on your applications?

A: As you know there are three rounds or deadlines for the applications. I took the GMAT in November, so I actually started writing over Thanksgiving. I sent some of the applications out in the January round and some in the March round. For Kellogg, it was due on March 15 and I sent it out March 14 by FEDEX! I intended to send out all of them by the second round. But Kellogg was one of my top choices so I wanted to make sure I got it right. By the time the second deadline came around I didn't feel comfortable with essays. But by the time I sent out the application to Kellogg I knew I had gotten into Anderson. I thought maybe I'd just go there. But then I decided to send my application out to Kellogg.

Q: What type of image did you try to portray in your essays.

A: I tried to portray a global image. I tried to stand out by emphasizing my background — my tricultural, trilingual, global image. In pretty much every single essay I made sure I write down tri-cultural, trilingual. And I leveraged that background by saying I could bring this diversity to business school.

Q: And then how did you pick the people that wrote your letters of recommendations for you?

A: Well, I came from a pretty small company, so it was not very convenient for me go to the president or the partners to say I needed a letter. I had to keep it confidential. It's not like the big companies, like in consulting, where everybody knows you're going to leave anyway. In the company where I worked it was different. It was small and I felt like if I leaked the information, people would treat me differently. So I wanted to make sure that I kept it confidential. So I went to two of my supervisors. I went to my prior supervisor, the media director, that I worked for two years, to ask for a letter. I also went to another superior who was not my direct supervisor. He was not a person I worked with on a day-to-day basis. He worked the East Coast and would assign projects to me. I worked on the West Coast and was in charge there. So I knew that he would not impact my work as much because he was stationed across the country. So I had some strategy on picking whom I wanted to confide in to write my letters. So I went to 2 superiors and schools that required a third letter, I went to a client.

Q: Why did you choose a client?

A: The reason I went to a client was the company that I worked for was very small. We only had about a total of 30 people nationwide. And I felt like most people applying for business school come from big companies. I had this small company complex. So I decided to go to a client from a big international corporation. Also on my resume I made sure I put my clients' names on it, and most of them were fortune 500 companies. So when people say okay this woman worked for a small company and we've never heard of it, but anyone would recognize the clients listed.

Q: Okay. And did you have any advisement during the process of the application?

A: Yes, I was lucky enough to have a friend who was a first year at the University Of Michigan. So he had already gone through the process, a year before me, and he actually lent me some of the books, gave me lots of advice, and also gave me contacts with other people attending business school. I was told I should talk to people attending the schools and get to know the cultures. So, for Michigan, I asked my friend to tell me what Michigan is all about. Then if I was asked in an interview or application about why I wanted to go to Michigan, I could write something that showed I knew about the school. So I didn't know a lot of people from other schools, but this friend of mine kind of gave me contacts — like email addresses from Wharton and Kellogg. So I wrote these people emails to gather information. Also I made sure I attended business school forums. These are forums that go around the country. They put on a business school fair and all the schools have a table or a booth and you go around and ask questions. So I made sure to ask at the booths what distinguishes your school from others. There were also some seminars for minorities. Admissions Officers would come in and talk to you about their school, to try to recruit you and give you a good look at their culture. Also, at Kaplan, the teachers would volunteer to answer any questions cause they've gone through the process. I relied a lot on friends.

Q: That's good. You had quite a network.

A: Really just one friend from Michigan, but because of him I kind of branched out to others. When I applied I had specific questions about my background and how I could relate my advertising background into business school, and this friend of mine had a very different background, so he referred me to somebody else who had a similar background, who goes to Michigan. Both of us had worked in marketing and so his advice helped me with my application. I recommend that applicants try to find people who have similar backgrounds that are attending business school. Seek out their advice. I think I got really good advice through emails, some people from Kellogg. They responded and gave me good advice. And then talk to schools, to get to know their cultures.

Q: Okay, now let's talk about your interviews. What did you try to achieve at your interviews?

A: I tried to be very consistent. I think in general I went to interviews before I wrote my essays. I was one of the last people to apply. I made sure I portrayed a very consistent image, like I told you, the global image. I had an idea of what I wanted to write on my application questions and so I tried to project the same image during the interview and the written application. I think they want to see consistency. You don't want to say, "I'm This" in the interview, and then on the essay say "I'm That." So even if people don't have their essays written, when they walk into these interviews they should already know how they will project themselves on the application and try to position themselves.

Q: Excellent. Okay, and after your application was complete did you send in any additional information?

A: Wharton put me on the waiting list, so I wrote them letters. And actually Kellogg originally gave me a deferred admission. They wanted me in but they had no more space and they actually said we'll give you a deferred admission and we want you to come next year. I didn't want to wait and if I had to wait I'd rather go to UCLA. So I wrote them a letter saying I really want to come to Kellogg, but that I thought I was ready for business school and didn't need another year of work experience. Also I told them that I had other schools waiting for my response. I got into Michigan and UCLA and was on the waiting list at Wharton. Originally when they called, they told me it was hard to change the deferred admission. They had given out 20 deferred admissions and they usually don't give you a chance to change that. If they want you to come in a year there's a reason. They said it was mostly because they want you to have more work experience, but I thought it was more because of when I applied. I sent them a letter explaining that I wanted to come this year and I followed up with a call and it worked. So I think they saw my endurance.

Q: Okay. Tell me what you are going to do this summer for your internship after your first year of business school?

A: I'm going to Procter and Gamble to work in Brand Management. I'm going to be working on feminine protection.

Q: Is there any other advice you would like to give to a person with a similar background applying to a top business school?

A: Essays are important. I spent a lot of time thinking what I really wanted to do with my life. The essay questions really make you think. They really make you think about your past and your future. So I probably never thought that much about what I did in my past or what growing up in Argentina meant to me. Subconsciously I might have known, but I never really thought of it in a logical way to actually put it down on paper, so it was a thought process, and that's gonna take a lot of time. So I tell people who are doing applications right now to start thinking about why they want to go to business school, and start thinking how their past shaped their personality. Everything you want to do in your life has to do with your past. So start thinking and putting those into kind of a framework. Because everybody takes it for granted. For example, I know I grew up in Argentina and spent time in Taiwan. I never really put them into how they shaped me into who I am now, and I think the essay questions really pushed me to think harder and deeper into who I am. It helps you realize who you want to be in the future. I think the hard part is to make yourself stand out from the crowd. So many people are applying to Business School.

Q: How do you do that?

A: For me it was easy because I think I had something to say about my background which I thought was rather unique. I'm sure every person would have something to say. If not maybe they want to start early on. You know, if you are thinking about applying to business school in two years, maybe you want to start doing something during those two years, so that they can stand out from the crowd. It doesn't have to be business related. It could be just a personal experience that is very different; it could change the way you look at the world. I think the admissions committee is looking at that type of diversity as well.

INTERVIEW: MICHAEL GOODMAN
Harvard Business School

Q: Can you tell me your name and your age?

A: Michael Goodman, age 27.

Q: Tell me about your education prior to business school?

A: I went to a public high school and then went to Duke University and got a BA in psychology.

Q: Besides your psychology degree what other types of activities did you participate in as an undergrad?

A: I was in a fraternity and I was president of the volunteer cancer patients work program.

Q: After you graduated, where did you go to work?

A: LEK Consulting in Boston.

Q: What type of consulting did you do?

A: Strategy, mergers and acquisitions.

Q: How long did you do that?

A: 4 years

Q: What positions did you have while you were there?

A: I started as an Associate, which is the first level as an undergrad and was promoted to Associate Consultant after 2 years and Consultant after about 3 1/2 years, which is an MBA position.

Q: So your career was going well. How did you decide to go back to business school?

A: In the consulting business, I felt like I knew enough. I was wondering how much further I could go there or anywhere else without an MBA. I just wanted to round out my business education.

Q: Had you already taken the GMAT?

A: I took it while I was working in Australia. I took it my third year of consulting.

Q: So you had some international experience as well?

A: Yes. I was in Australia.

Q: What type of projects did you work on?

A: Privatizing the Australian airports.

Q: Did you end up taking a review course at all for the GMAT?

A: No, I used the Kaplan book but I didn't take the course.

Q: How long did you study for?

A: Probably about 2 or 3 months.

Q: In a pretty organized fashion or just as you could?

A: Every weekend I would do a practice test, and then I just did the sections in the book each night as I had time.

Q: Which schools did you end up applying to?

A: Harvard, Stanford, Wharton and Kellogg.

Q: How did you pick them?

A: Those were just the top 4.

Q: Tell me a little bit about your applications? You had a pretty diverse background with a non-business undergrad, but then a solid business experience. What type of image did you try to project?

A: That the team and its results are always number one. I made sure that I gave them a rounded story about what I have done and where I want to go.

Q: Do you remember some of the specifics that you tried to put into your essays?

A: Specifically, my leadership experience at work and at school. I was very focused on working in the future in marketing in the biotech field, and I linked my past work experiences to my experience within the field of cancer.

Q: Through your volunteer experience?

A: Yes, I had also taken some time off to work with this cancer program when I came back from Australia before going back to work at LEK.

Q: What did you end up doing for them?

A: I wrote a brochure for parents who have kids with cancer to help explain to the disease to their children and help them manage their lives. I did the endowment fund raising strategy for the program. I really liked the organization. It was a good break from consulting.

Q: How did you pick the people to write your letters of recommendation and who where they?

A: I picked an art history professor whom I took for 4 years in school. I also chose partners and managers at work who I had worked with throughout my years at LEK.

Q: Did you have much advisement from either peers or people that had gone to these different schools that you were applying to during your process?

A: My sister who graduated from HBS in '98 was my primary editor. I also had help from friends who had been to graduate school.

Q: How did you get information about the programs that you were applying to?

A: I just ordered the information that they had and I went to visit Wharton and Kellogg. I spoke to people who went to the other two schools.

Q: It sounds like you managed to stay involved with the cancer program. Were you involved with other extracurricular activities while working?

A: Yes. I was active with the Duke alumni group in Boston and I also worked with an organization called Gaining Ground which was volunteer gardening in suburban Boston — helping with gardens where the foods went to local shelters and low cost produce.

Q: Did you go to the schools for the interviews or did you do alumni interviews?

A: I went to the schools for Wharton and Kellogg. Stanford doesn't interview and I didn't have an interview at Harvard.

Q: How did you feel those went and do you remember any impressions you had of those different interviews?

A: Kellogg interview went really well. I felt like it would be a good place. I thought the Wharton interview was actually sort of rough because I got zero feedback. It was a very unique situation because my interviewer was actually a very good friend, and she was just a year ahead of me in college and I knew a lot about her. It was strange. You have to do the interview very straight-faced and very professional. It was your standard interview, with the standard questions such as about your leadership experiences...

Q: After your interviews, did you sent any additional information to update your application?

A: No.

Q: How did you decide which school to go to?

A: It really came down to brand. I felt like that the education was a little different at each school with some things being good and some things being bad at each. But I got the impression from other applicants at the top schools that Harvard was their first choice. I felt that if people in the business community felt that way too, then I should just go for it and have the extra edge. It wasn't actually my first choice in terms of the type and quality of the education, but it turned out to be a very good choice and I actually like it a lot more than I thought it would and I am getting a lot more out of it than I would have thought.

Q: Is there any further advice that you would like to give to someone like yourself?

A: You have to weave a tale in your application. That is what a partner I worked with told people who were applying. And that's very true that you have to give a consistent story about yourself. Make it seem like you know exactly who you are, where you are from and why you want to go to business school and what differences you can make at that school and whether or not you actually believe you are going to do what you say you are going to do. You have to provide an integrated story about yourself.

Q: With your background, how do you think that business school will benefit you? Has your opinion changed of what you are getting from your MBA since you have been there?

A: I feel that I am getting a little more out of it than I thought I was going to get. It is more of a rounding out of my business knowledge. I now know a little more about operations, strategy, management and marketing.

Q: Tell me a little bit about your internship?

A: Basically the position coming out of business school is a marketing manager at Clorox and I am working on a new brand called Fresh Care. I am also working in a couple of execution-type promotion projects and simple strategy projects.

INTERVIEW: ARTI FINN
Kellogg Graduate School of Management

Q: Can you tell me your name and age?

A: Arti Finn and I am 29.

Q: Can you tell me about your undergraduate education?

A: I went to Kenyon College. It is a small liberal arts school in Ohio. I studied English and Political Science.

Q: Did you participate in any significant extracurricular activities while you were there?

A: Yes, I worked on the school newspaper. I was treasurer of the rugby club. I was the editor for the Conservative Magazine and then I did a lot of fun stuff outside of that.

Q: After you graduated, where did you go to work?

A: I tried to take some time off and I went to Montana and I worked as a housekeeper.

Q: How long did you do that?

A: About 4 months and then my parents said that was not the reason we sent you to college. So I decided to explore my roots since I was half Indian and half American. My mother is from India, so I decided I wanted to go there and check things out. I went there and was a reporter for an Indian magazine called India Today. It is the largest Indian magazine.

Q: Is it in English?

A: It is in English and also in 5 dialects of Hindi. I worked on the English version.

Q: Did you get to travel around India reporting?

A: I didn't travel. I did most of my reporting from Delhi. I covered tourism and business stuff mostly.

Q: How long did you do that?

A: I did that for one-and-a-half years.

Q: Where did you go from there?

A: I am from DC and I went back to DC and I worked as a political reporter for a newsletter. It is a political newsletter called The Hotline and I was a political reporter covering the 1994 election. I did all the writing from DC, but I had contacts all over the country. I often worked from 4:30 a.m. until 9:00 p.m. or 10:00 p.m.

Q: Then after that?

A: I am a very non-traditional business student. After that, I decided I hated being a
political reporter and I did not like the kind of writing where I was just writing constantly and never reading again what I wrote. I was offered a position with an educational publishing company in NY City where I did corporate relations. I worked for the head of Corporate Relations and I was in charge of the corporate relations program for the company. I did a lot of work with our lobbyist in DC.

Q: Did you apply to business school from that position?

A: I did that for almost 2 years and while I was there I applied to business school.

Q: When did you take your GMAT?

A: I took them in the fall when I was applying.

Q: Did you take any review courses?

A: Yes. I took the Princeton Review. I am a very bad test taker and I did very badly on the GMAT. For some reason they let me in.

Q: Did the Princeton Review help though?

A: I did. I think that I got a 590, the low end.

Q: Would you study the same way with the Princeton Review again if you had to do it again?

A: Yes, I loved the Princeton Review. I think it was excellent. Unfortunately, it just couldn't help me. When I first started taking the test, I was in the 400's, so it definitely improved me. I didn't think I would actually get into business school with a test score like that, but for some reason Kellogg didn't mind.

Q: How did you choose the schools that you were going to apply to and how many did you apply to?

A: I applied to four schools. I chose my schools based on how flexible they were with their curriculum. I am very interested in education and business and so I wanted a school that had a good school of education as well as a business school. I applied to Kellogg, Columbia, Stanford and Vanderbilt. Vanderbilt was my back-up, but they rejected me. My applying experience is very bizarre. I loved Kellogg when I came out here. I had a good friend who was a second year here. He and his friends were so nice to me when I came to visit. I decided this was the school for me.

Q: Tell me a little bit about your applications. Obviously, you had a diverse background. What type of image did you try to project in your essays?

A: I think my essays really helped me out the most and I think probably are the reasons why I got in. As I said before, I was writer so that really helped. I approached my essays as a more creative event than I think most people did. One of my favorite essays that I actually turned into an article after I got into school was about all the different pairs of shoes I have worn in my life and how there is a cliché for these (i.e. to walk a mile in another man's moccasins). Since I was half Indian and half American, I have this unique ability to fit in to different cultures in a way that other people don't necessary have. People will look at me and think I am Spanish, or whatever. I think that was Kellogg's core essay ("what would you add to the school"), so I wrote an essay about that. They wanted to know why I wanted to come to business school and I had a very clear vision of what I wanted to get out business school. I had a backup in education. I knew a lot about that. I knew a lot about government because I was a reporter but I really didn't know anything about business and I think to succeed in the education industry, you need a background in all three (education, business, and government). So I wanted business school to round me out. In college, I hadn't taken any business classes. I didn't even take an economics class, so I didn't know anything about it. I worked very hard while I was here at Kellogg. More than most people. A lot of people came here to have fun for two years and take a break from their hectic, consulting, investment banking lives. That wasn't my goal at all.

Q: How did you think that business school is going to help you?

A: It has already helped me so much. Just in terms of doing stuff in the education world, I have gained so many more contacts. I had a lot of contacts that were professors, etc., but coming here I had most of the pre-eminent people in the education industry come to give presentations at Kellogg. We had a conference that was great. It was so good that Merrill Lynch approached us this spring and they stated that they wanted to work with us to make this conference bigger next year. Those contacts were invaluable. I got great job offers. I have so many opportunities to meet so many amazing people. That includes the students too. I met so many people here who I am going to try keep in touch with for my entire life. I feel that I have gotten more out of business school than most because I didn't know anything going in. I used this an opportunity to educate myself with all the stuff that I had been missing out on for so long.

Q: How did you pick the people to write your letters of recommendation and who were they?

A: Actually Kellogg only asks you for one. It was my boss at Scholastic that I asked to write me a recommendation. One, because he was someone who really encouraged me to apply to school and two, because he and I had this very unique relationship in that it was almost like we were father and daughter. I use to hang out with him and his family on the weekends. He really went out of his way to be really nice to me. We still keep in touch. He was the perfect person to write my letter of recommendation for me.

Q: Did you have any others for the other schools?

A: I had my boss at the Hotline when I worked as a political reporter. She was excellent. She wrote me a very good recommendation. I also had another one of the executive vice-presidents at Scholastic write me a letter of recommendation for Stanford. I had a very diverse group. I think the one that was the most important was my direct supervisor.

Q: Did you choose the others for their position?

A: I chose my boss at the Hotline because she knew how hard I had worked there. It was a good indication of my determination to do things in adverse conditions. The other one I chose because of her position and her connections. I only used that one for one business school. The other thing that helped me out was that my roommate in NY was also applying to business school. We read each other's essays and we were both really encouraging to each other. I think that made a lot of difference for me. It improved my motivation.

Q: How did you find out more about the schools that you were applying to?

A: I had friends who had gone to business school, so I definitely tapped into that network. I talked to older people whom my parents knew who had gone to business school. Before I even applied, I talked to people to find out if this was the right thing to do because I thought that I should go to the school of education. Business school is definitely a way for you to learn a lot about the business world in a short period of time. After being at business school, I realized that I would have never known half this stuff even if I had continued working for the next 6 years. It is amazing how much I have learned.

Q: What type of things?

A: Specific tools such as ways of examining problems. I can approach any sort of business issue now with information that I learned in business school.

Q: Prior to business school did you participate in any activities outside of work?

A: Actually I taught a class once a week. It was a government class. I volunteered in a public school and I taught high school students. It was nice, because it was my boss' son who taught the class so I could go once a week and just teach different topics. I taught everything from how to use the Internet to how to use our lobbyists, etc. I did some benefit type stuff in NY. That was more social than anything.

Q: Did you have an interview a Kellogg?

A: Yes, on campus. I think that made a lot of difference actually with my application. I think the two reasons I got in were one, my interview and two, my essays. I had the unique background and the reason why I wanted to go. Kellogg really looks for that. They don't want every investment banker that has ever been around. They look for diversity.

Q: What in your interview made it so good?

A: My interviewer was actually really interested in education. He was on the board of a school. I think that helped. He also specifically interviewed the more diverse candidates and I think that helped. I talked a lot about education and why I thought the industry needed business people. Showing up on campus tells them that you really want to go.

Q: So how did you decide on Kellogg?

A: It was the only school I was accepted to. I didn't even apply to places like Harvard or Wharton because the image was just so contrary to what kind of person I am. I am social but I work hard. I think that exemplifies Kellogg. I am different. I applied to Columbia and I know now that if I had ever gone there, I would have been miserable. You work hard at Kellogg, but it is not like you can't do other stuff on the side. For all of fall term, I only really did my conference. I spent 40 hours a week doing that.

Q: What did you do for your internship after your first year of business school?

A: I worked at Time-Warner. I worked for the guy who was in charge of new product development at Time. Then he left, so they offered me his job, so I took that.

Q: Do you have any additional advice for someone with a similar background to yourself?

A: Take advantage of the way you can convey your message in your essays. Kellogg takes it very seriously. They read your application extremely carefully. I heard that after my roommate worked on the admissions committee. A lot of people think the essays don't matter, but I think they matter a lot more than people think. I think that is the reason why I got in. I had a friend who was applying here and she did not put a lot effort into her essays. She was a perfect candidate. She had a great GMAT, great grades, very diverse and she spent a lot of time in Europe, etc., but she did not get in. Definitely interview on campus. I think business schools are looking for more diverse candidates not just ethically but also in terms of work experience. That is very important. If you are really interested in going to business school, show them that you want to do something besides being a banker.

INTERVIEW: HOMERO GONZALEZ
Kellogg Graduate School of Management

Q: Can you tell me your name and your age?

A: Homero Gonzalez and my age is 27.

Q: Can you tell me about your education prior to business school?

A: I'm an international student from Mexico and received my college degree in Mexico. I chose to be an industrial engineer in part because it did not require you to commit to a specific discipline and it was a mix of management and engineering. I started in a private university of Monterrey, Mexico which is my hometown. I supported myself in college through scholarships and work.

Q: After you graduated, where did you go to work?

A: I went to work at a small subsidiary of a very large cement company, the third largest cement company in the world. It is based in Monterrey, Mexico and is a very prestigious company in Mexico. I started working in the Logistic Department, then worked as head of the Marketing Department for the subsidiary, and, finally, ended up in the Planning Department.

Q: How many years did you work for the cement company?

A: 4 1/2 years.

Q: So your career was going great and you were doing well with this company. How did you make the decision that you wanted to go back to business school?

A: I am the kind of person who benefits from formal education — I do well in that kind of environment. Before business school I tried to research the different university graduate programs. I looked into everything from psychology, engineering and management. After having some experiences in my work and in the non-profit areas where I worked, I realized that I was most interested in management. My company in Mexico is known for giving scholarships if you are accepted to one of the top 10 business schools in the U.S. So I applied to three of the top business schools. I studied for my GMAT and for my TOEFL exam, which is also a big deal in international applications. (TOEFL is the English exam.) After I got very promising scores on my GMAT and my TOEFL, I decided to tell the people in my company that I was going to apply.

Q: How did you go about studying for your tests, the GMAT and the TOEFL? Where you able to take review courses?

A: For the TOEFL, I had the opportunity to take one of the practice exams. For maybe a week, I studied for two hours a day and listened to CNN Headline News in English on an AM band in Mexico. I also became an expert in filling in bubbles. I got an almost perfect score on the TOEFL exam, even though I didn't have that much practice in English at all. This is why I didn't want them to interview me because I couldn't speak English that well at the time. For the GMAT, I took the Princeton Review Course. It is very helpful if you are an international student because you get acquainted to the American style of questions. I improved my score from 490 to 690 in the 2 months that I was studying for the GMAT.

Q: Was the GMAT available in Monterrey?

A: Yes, I took the GMAT in Monterrey. I also took the Princeton review course in Monterrey. Monterrey sends, maybe, the second largest number of students to the United States for MBA's from Mexico. It is the third largest city in Mexico.

Q: You said you applied to three schools, how did you choose those three?

A: I chose the schools by their ranking, by the references of friends, and by their brochures. I did not have the opportunity of visiting them as many people do. I was trying to get an understanding of what they were like from a third-person viewpoint.

Q: Did you speak to people who had gone to Kellogg?

A: Some of the people I talked to had gone to Kellogg and some had not, but they all talked about the team-oriented environment of Kellogg, an environment where everybody helps everybody. Kellogg is known for its supportive atmosphere. It is similar to my college experience and my prior working experience. The university where I studied, the Catholic University in Monterrey, also has this humanistic feel of education. So Kellogg was a good fit for me.

Q: What were the other two schools that you applied to?

A: Wharton and Stanford. My first choice was Stanford, most of all because the CEO of my company was a Stanford grad. Being a Stanford grad in Monterrey is like having blue blood — it helps to impress recruiters, especially in my company where some of the top officials, especially the CEO, are Stanford grads and distinguished alumni. My second choice was Kellogg. Stanford did not accept me, but I was accepted at Kellogg. My third choice was Wharton.

Q: Tell me a little bit about your application. Obviously, you have a unique background. What did you try to stress in your applications?

A: I realized that I had three unique areas in my background. First was my school experience, second was my work experience, and third was my part-time job in a non-profit organization. I tried to have everything fit into one picture. It was like making a model. You have to use the information you have about yourself to build this model. You have to realize the limitations inherent in the model, but at the same time make the pieces of your background work well together. I tried to do this with my school experience, my work experience and my work with the non-profit. After I completed the essays in this manner, I had some of my friends review them for me. I also asked the help from some English Professors, and a cousin of mine here in the U.S., who is a practically an American, to review all the grammar, etc.

Q: Did that help significantly?

A: Yes. It helped a lot. Also writing in another language helps you to be more concise. English is different from Spanish because you are not just writing different words, you are almost saying different things. Although I had some help with grammar, as I said before, I did not ask for too much help because I wanted the people who were reading the essays to realize that I was an international student because many schools look at the applications blindfolded to the name. I realized that this was an advantage for me. For example, I mentioned something about Mexico and something about being an international student. Therefor, the application was unblinded by the content of my essay.

Q: I wanted to ask you about your extracurricular activities. You talked about a non-profit organization that you worked with. Can you tell me a little more about that?

A: I got involved in the second year of college. It was a young organization, which looked to improve the quality of life of disabled persons. I worked there during the summer. They were growing a lot in size from a program helping 40 handicapped people using 60 volunteers to an operation of 300 disabled persons and 400 volunteers. They work in different areas of Mexico. It was a very interesting organization. They had a lot of people eager to volunteer, but lacked a staff with managerial experience. I had the opportunity of applying some of my formal education. I started to do different things with them and I ended up writing a book with one of the founders of the organization about the experiences of young volunteers meeting for the first time with people who have some type disabilities and then the experiences they shared.

Q: Did you publish that book?

A: When the organization celebrated its 10 year anniversary, they sold 2,000 hardcopies of the book. It was fun.

Q: When you were working with the organization, where you working mainly to improve the managerial side or working directly with the disabled?

A: I started working with persons with disabilities and then ended up as a coordinator. First I worked with the volunteers. Then I was a counselor. Then the next time I was called a consultant. I started to be assigned to specific projects. For example, I worked on fund raising from international organizations. Also, I managed task assignment to new volunteers. It was over a 7-year period. I hope to go back to this organization.

Q: Did you have alumni interviews or did you go to the schools?

A: I have a very unique situation. I was very scared in the interview especially because I had little experience in speaking English. I called to ask for an interview. They took my information and then I got a letter telling me that my interview had been waved as there were too many applicants to be able to interview everyone. Fortunately, I was accepted.

Q: Did you interview at the other schools that you applied to?

A: No. Stanford doesn't like interviews and Wharton does not do interviews in Mexico. At that time, I did not have the money to fly to the schools.

Q: After you completed your applications did you send any additional information to update your application?

A: No

Q: Where are you doing your internship this summer?

A: I am sponsored by the cement company and so am going back to work with them in a different area.

Q: What area are you going to work in?

A: The supervisor that I was assigned to is the Development Director of the company. He supervises human resources, energy and some other areas so I will work for him. After I graduate, I have to go back to them and work for 4 years. I would never have been able to get the $100,000 that I needed to pay for my MBA education without the business scholarship because I don't come from a wealthy family. I really feel that working for them for 4 years in a decent position is more than enough for me.

Q: If you were to give any other advice to someone coming from a similar international background, is there anything that you would like to add?

A: Try to learn as much as possible about the language that people use in business school. I didn't know any of the MBA buzzwords, like what an IPO is or who McKinsey or Goldman Sachs are. Just like its important to learn English, it's important to learn the language of business for the MBA profession and for the MBA culture. I think everyone applying should learn more about the MBA culture of business in the US.

INTERVIEW: BRYAN BOCHES
Wharton School of Business

Q: Tell me your name and your age?

A: My name is Bryan Boches and I'm 29.

Q: Where did you go to undergrad?

A: University of California Santa Barbara.

Q: What did you major in there?

A: Accounting and Economics.

Q: Did you participate in any big activities while you were an undergrad?

A: Water polo.

Q: After you graduated, where did you go to work?

A: I worked at a startup called University Painting Professionals. I did that for about 8 months, crashed and burned. We have a few problems and did not agree on things. I went to healthcare consulting for one year in Canada and in San Francisco and after that I went to Asia with Morgan Stanley and worked all over Asia.

Q: What type of projects did you work on in Asia?

A: I did IPO's and acquisitions. I worked on Beijing Enterprise's IPO, which was a big subscribed deal, with hoards of people lined up outside all the office buildings trying to get subscriptions. It was like Amazon's IPO, and everyone knowing that it was Amazon. The stock went up 6 times in the first day and it was craziness. It was like the Internet. Then I worked in Beijing for a while and in Hong Kong for a while, then was staffed in Australia, Indonesia, Thailand and India.

Q: How long did you do that?

A: Three and a half years.

Q: So...you are having all this fun with work, going around the world. How did you make the decision to go back to business school?

A: It was really tough to go back. I could have stayed with the job and not gone back, since there was no reason to go back. The reason I chose to go back was largely because of the advice I got from people that I respected, people who said that, just as a life experience, they were glad that they went to school. I view my life as a string of experiences and I felt that if I didn't go to school, I was not going primarily for the reason that I wanted to make money faster and I thought that this was probably a weak perspective.

Q: When did you take the GMAT?

A: I took it during my second year of work while in Hong Kong.

Q: When you where there, were you able to take any review course?

A: Yes, they had one when you were working. However, working at Morgan Stanley, you don't get a lot of time. I did take a Princeton review course. We traveled all the time so I didn't get to go to the classes. I had that little study guidebook and everyone uses that thing.

Q: What schools did you end up applying to and how did you pick them?

A: Wharton, Stanford and Harvard. I picked them because they were the top three.

Q: Besides the rank, were you looking at the culture of the schools?

A: First off, I went to Santa Barbara as an undergrad. My parents did not give any direction to me about where to go. So I went to the school that I thought was cool. I thought it was a fun school with the beach. I was a water polo guy. I loved it. It was a beautiful school and I felt comfortable there. You don't realize how much harder it was to get a job out of that school than it would have been out of other schools. When I thought about business school...the reasons you go to business school are for the breadth of contacts and for the reputation and learning from that school. So I think it is pretty wise for you to go to the best school that you can go to. So I ranked the schools as Stanford, Harvard and Wharton, but I did not get into Stanford or Harvard.

Q: Tell me about your applications. You had a great story to tell with a variety of experiences. What kind of image did you try to project onto your application and your essays?

A: I tried to game the system, to be honest. I probably overly tried to game it. Looking back, I would say that the schools are surprisingly different and actually the admissions committees are a little bit different at looking at individuals. However, it makes no sense to try to game anything in your essays because it comes out. It is better to just reveal who you are and answer the questions honestly than try to answer the questions in the way you think that they want to answer the questions, which a lot of people do. What I ended up doing was writing real serious essays for Harvard and then I wrote tender essays for Stanford. For Wharton, I decided to write a parable about Jack and the Beanstalk and just have a good time with it. I was thinking I took the other essays too seriously and that I would rather be creative on this one. They take a long time to write.

Q: It sounds great, the creativity paid off obviously.

A: I guess so. I think it is a pretty random process. I don't attest to my writing skills to getting into school. I have no idea how they make these decisions.

Q: Did you have any advisement through any of your process of application (such as from peers, faculty, etc.)?

A: No. The only person that looked at my essay was my sister. I will say that after going to school and seeing the admissions process you learn what is important to the school. As an applicant, you can get a huge benefit from having someone who was at the school look at your resume and also give you recommendations. Current students can have real insight and I didn't realize that when I was applying. For example, at Wharton, students can put in a word for you. They have impact. You are an existing student. You can affect the admissions process. The school listens to its existing student base. If you know a lot of people at the school and they strongly support of you, it will make a difference.

Q: How did you go about picking the people to write your letter of recommendations?

A: I picked the people from work who knew me the best. I think it is less important to get the biggest guy unless that big guy really is connected to the school. There are some guys who actually can really pull slots at the school and it is real. They can almost pull you a slot. They can't completely do it. They can raise some eyebrows if you qualify. You always want to go for the top guy, but it makes no sense to go for that guy if he doesn't even know you or if you hadn't done any real work with him. You need to have someone who really knows you.

Q: As far as any extracurricular activities, did you have any time to do any? I know you were working a lot.

A: I played water polo in Hong Kong and traveled on a basketball team throughout China. It was made of some ex-pros from Taiwan and Australia and some diplomatic people and people from different companies. We were supposedly on an economic mission playing different provinces. We did one or two deals for people in the provinces. It was just a lot of fun.

Q: How long did you do that for?

A: For about 1 year and then I played water polo in Hong Kong. I did a bunch of activities. I did not do anything for the most part in the community. It was very difficult to work in the community in Asia. They don't have a standard charity system set up there or nonprofit organization system. It doesn't work that way out there.

Q: As for your interviews for business school, did you do alumni interviews or visit the schools?

A: I did one with Harvard and I decided to do it via phone. I guess half the applicants get in who make the interview process. I would not recommend doing the interview on the phone, especially overseas.

Q: Was there another way that you could have pulled it off?

A: I could have gone out there and just made it happen. I should have done that if it was important to me.

Q: After the interviews, did you send any additional information to update your application?

A: No.

Q: What did you do for your internship after your first year?

A: I worked at Fidelity and did some debt trading.

Q: And now after graduation what do you plan to do?

A: I am trying to do a start up right now. We have just gone through our VC round evaluation and received some offers.

Q: In what field?

A: Internet.

Q: If you were to give advice to someone similar to yourself about applying to a top school that you haven't already mentioned, what would it be?

A: My advice would be to not wait until the last second because you know you will. Do your essays early. When your re-read your essays you will just find a million things you want to change. You will learn a lot more about the school and you will have time to think about it and add to your essays. It will turn out a thousand times better than if you do the night before the deadline, which I did every time.

Kellogg Graduate School of Management

Q: Tell me your name and your age.

A: My name is Sean Walter. I just turned thirty-one.

Q: And can you tell me a little about your undergraduate education?

A: I went to Williams College, which is in northwestern Massachusetts. I was an English major. I did not take a whole lot of analytical coursework, which was basically a choice that I made because I had done a lot of that during high school and did not feel like continuing down that path at that time. I studied abroad my junior year at Oxford University, Exeter College. Williams actually has an exchange program with them, so that's how I got into that. Also, towards the end of my college career I focused pretty heavily on comparative religion as opposed to literature.

Q: And besides your academics, what kind of extracurriculars did you participate in?

A: I was a DJ on the college radio station. When I was at Oxford, I rowed crew. The first couple of years at Williams I was on the Ultimate Frisbee team. And that's probably about it.

Q: And after you graduated, where did you end up going to work?

A: I ended up working at Monitor. I actually took a job with them in their desktop publishing department, at the time thinking that I wanted to be a graphic designer. And I didn't have any formal training so that was a way to get some basic experience. But pretty quickly that evolved into a much more computer and technology position for me. So, I ended up doing MIS stuff for them, working on a couple of fairly big internal projects. One was an attempt to develop a multi-media tool for doing competitive diagnosis of our clients' companies, which was a six-month project

131

that never really got off the ground. And then the two other big projects, one was actually trying to redesign the interactions of the processes that took place between the desktop publishing department and the rest of the firm. That was about an eighteen-month project. And one of the outputs of that project was that the firm needed a group to do graphic design and web site development. So, in my last couple of years there I set up that group, which was almost like starting a new business. We actually had to write up a business plan and present it to the founders of the company and then were essentially charged with developing a client base of our own both inside and outside the company.

Q: So, that was a substantial project. Did you end up leaving in the middle of it?

A: We had it up and running for about six months by the time I left Monitor. But I had been doing the work in one form or another for more like twelve to eighteen months.

Q: Okay. And how did you decide to go back to business school with your background?

A: It was actually during the first couple of months, when we were talking about starting this business up. We were throwing around a bunch of ideas and starting to craft the business plan and I realized that I was having a lot of fun doing that. And then on top it off, my girlfriend was in business school at the time and she would come home and talk about the stuff that she was doing and I realized that I was really enjoying those conversations. I was also enjoying putting together the business plan for this graphic design and web development group. And so those two things in combination kind of suggested that I should at least get my feet wet, take the GMAT, talk to some people about what this whole business school thing is and things just kept moving from there.

Q: So, when did you end up taking the GMAT?

A: I took the last written test in June of '97.

Q: And did you take any review courses?

A: No. ETS publishes a book of sample tests that I got. So I had a book of sample tests, and again it was one of those things, that I said okay, I will do a couple of these sample tests and if I do okay on them, then I am not going to bother with a review course. And I did fine on them.

Q: So, did you continue to study on your own?

A: No. I did a couple of the review tests and I was doing fine on them, and I just didn't bother doing anything more than that. There really wasn't any reason to.

Q: And when you got down to choosing your schools, how did you choose what schools you would apply to?

A: It was a little bit tough because I was living in Boston and would have liked to go to one of the Boston schools like Harvard or Sloan, but I didn't get in. I did get into Babson in Boston, and actually got a   pretty attractive scholarship from them. But I had to really make decisions about whether I wanted to improve my life and go to a really good school, or did I want to stay in Boston and not go into much debt and kind of maintain my life, but not go to a school with quite the reputation. And in the end, I made my decision based on reputation and it was after talking with a whole bunch of people who basically said that reputation was a huge driver of how employers look at you after business school.

Q: And did you apply to others around the country?

A: Yes. Because my work background was a little non-traditional, certainly compared to most of the business school applicants coming out of Monitor. And so I applied to eight schools. I basically picked top schools with a couple of back-ups thrown in.

Q: And as far as your applications, coming from this non-traditional background, what image did you try to project onto your applications for business school?

A: That's a really good question. I tried to leverage my entrepreneurial experience in setting up the graphic design and web business at Monitor, so that was one of the big things I did. The other was that I actually made concerted effort to make my essays really personal because some of the research I had done on schools led me to think the admissions people want to get to know you. And on top of that, I took the approach that I wanted to go to a school that's going to appreciate me for who I am and not for who I presented myself to be in my essays. Some people may say that is a little fatalistic, but essentially I did a good job of being explicit about who I was, where I was coming from, and why this was important to me. And I took a hard look at each of the schools and what they had to offer, and talked specifically about how each of those fit with my own personality. So in that sense there is a little of putting the cart before the horse. I tried to pick the schools I was going to apply to and made their offerings personal to me

Q: Do you have any thoughts about the timing of your application?

A: I actually tried to meet the first deadline for all the schools. Looking back I would probably do that again, but I would actually start my process earlier. As it was, I didn't really have letters to my recommenders until fairly late in that game. And so, I think I started downloading applications and used the software application that you can get that allows you to do all the generic data simultaneously. But, I didn't really start that process until October 1st. And some of the applications were due mid to late November.

Q: You talked briefly about your recommendations, how did you choose who to write those for you?

A: If I had to do it again, I would probably do it a little bit differently. But, I basically wanted to maximize the combination of the recommenders knowing a lot about me and the recommenders carrying some weight within their organization. Basically, all the recommenders were people at Monitor, all the ones I chose. And two of them were people whom I had worked with pretty closely. In fact, one was someone whom I had had a falling out with a couple years prior who was also the subject of one of my essays for a couple of schools. Another was the person who co-founded the graphic design group with me. I had those two people I had worked with very closely. There was my co-founder, who was the global manager of Monitor desktop publishing, so that is a little bit prestigious. The other person whom I had worked with very closely was Monitor's Chief Information Officer, so that carried some weight. And then the last person was someone whom I actually had not worked quite as closely with. I had worked closely with him on a couple of projects and he was a global account manager for the firm, which is kind of just below what is essentially partnership level. So, he had some weight as well, and also was more on the professional side of the firm as opposed to the administrative side of the firm. Looking back, I probably would have left him out and would have picked someone more at my level that had worked with me really closely. I think I would have gotten a stronger recommendation from a peer than from this person who had worked closely with me and respected me, but I didn't have a tight, tight relationship with him.

Q: Did you have much advisement during this process of application?

A: Not really. I showed my essays to a couple of friends and in some cases believed in their feedback and in other cases did not. I kept it quiet at Monitor because I was working on this other relatively high risk project with the new business and if people knew potentially I was going to be leaving before it was really up and running I might have lost some credibility there.

Q: So you kept kind of tight lipped about that?

A: Yeah. But I think that there are plenty of people at Monitor who do seek out advice especially when it is sort of an expectation that most people in the firm will go back to school.

Q: During your whole work experience, did you participate in extra-curricular activities as well?

A: Yeah, I did actually. I did a couple things on a personal level and a couple things more on a community level. I've been a pretty avid fiction writer for a number of years and was actually just starting to try and get published around the time I was applying to business schools. I sort of made a deal with myself that I would try to do both simultaneously and if I got published before I got into business school then that would be a sign from God or something. But, I'm in business school, because I didn't get published. Business school is really crazy, so it is hard to find the time, but I spend maybe on average an hour a week right now writing. I also started learning how to play piano and that was through a music school, where I started taking a somewhat community involved role. The school where I was taking lessons was a non-profit, very community-oriented organization and I basically said what can I do for these people; I can give them a web site. So, I did that. Also, there were a couple of years when I was tutoring people in English as a second language. And then I did a pro-bono graphic design project in between undergrad and business school.

Q: I know that you went on an interview for Kellogg. Did you interview at other schools?
A: Yes. Of the eight schools that I applied to, I interviewed with four. I interviewed at Babson, Kellogg, University of Chicago, and the Sloan School (MIT).

Q: And do you remember how you tried to portray yourself at the interviews and what they asked you that was good and what you asked them that was good?

A: Well, I have pretty strong memories of my Sloan interview because it didn't go very well. They asked me about my career history, kind of what have you done. And I went into way too much detail there, I used up a lot of the interview time because I've got a weird sort of a career history that is hard to summarize. I wasn't really prepared for that question even though it may seem pretty obvious that it would come up. And then also I got questions there about leadership within the Monitor organization and what I had done. I did not have questions like that in any other interview; the others were much more laid back. This one was much more like a job interview. And it was also my last one, which was also why I wasn't that prepared. I was prepared for questions like why do you want to go to school X? And why you over somebody else and what will you bring to the school. I was prepared for all that, but I was not prepared for why did you make the career decisions you made, what sort of leadership roles have you taken within your company, those kinds of things.

Q: So, would you give advice to prepare for the interviews?

A: Yeah, I think that it is kind of a good idea no matter what. I also focused my essays on things other than specific company experiences, so I wasn't really prepared there either. Some applicants talk a lot about their work. For Kellogg, where I got in, one of my essays was specifically about work and everything else was not, or at least not directly.

Q: Did you send additional information to update your applications after your interviews?

A: No. I did not. Typically with my interviews, which in almost every case were alumni interviews off campus, I would send a thank you note and sometimes in the thank you note would supplement stuff we had talked about in conversation. But, I never sent in additional stuff to the admissions offices.

Q: Are you a first or second year?

A: I'm a first year.

Q: So, do you know what you are going to do this summer in you internship?

A: I got an internship through what is called the Kaufman entrepreneur intern program, which is run by the Ewing May Kaufman foundation in Kansas City. It is a foundation, which was set up to promote education and entrepreneurship. So, they are sponsoring me to work with a Chicago area start up company and the company is called Dynamic Trade and they do e-commerce. They are sort of an outsourcing service for companies that want to do e-commerce.

Q: That's an exciting area these days. Especially staying in Chicago, not going to Palo Alto.

A: There is actually a lot going on here, or more than I expected when I was applying.

Q: Is there is anything else you would like to add, some general advice to someone similar to yourself?

A: I would say a couple things. One is present yourself as somebody who is comfortable with who you are, both who you are and why you are going to business school. I was definitely applying late in life relative to a lot of people and I never really addressed that issue in my essays and I assume that that helped me more than it hurt me. In fact I did address it in my Kellogg essay talking about the fact that two or three years ago there was no way that business school would have made sense for me either on a personal or on a professional level. In that sense, I talked about how I had gone through a maturing process that was probably delayed over what a lot of people had gone through.

Q: The main thing is being honest with both you and the admissions board, to say this really is who I am, this is what I really what I want to do, I am not making this up. I know a lot of people get here and they say they want to go into consulting but didn't write it in their essays. If what you want to do is be a consultant, I actually think you can write a stronger essay if you are up front about that, rather than making up reasons why you want to be a green peace financial manager.

INTERVIEW: ERICA BLEWER
Wharton School of Business

Q: Tell me your name and age.

A: Erica Blewer, age 25.

Q: Tell me about your education prior to business school.

A: I did my undergraduate work at the University of Texas at Austin. It had a good Liberal Arts program called Plan II within the Liberal Arts degree. Plan II is an honors Liberal Arts program that has been at University of Texas (UT) for years. It is a general degree, but with small classes and very good professors. That was were I started thinking about going into business someday, but that a true Liberal Arts education wouldn't float. Fortunately, UT also had a good business major, which I started in my second year of college as a sophomore. I applied to the honors business program within the College of Business. I then added finance as a third major in my senior year. In all, I finished with a BA in Plan II and BBA in the honors business program and in finance in 1995 and started Wharton in 1998.

Q: While you were an undergrad, what other activities did you participate in?

A: I was involved with several different clubs and organizations. I was the President of an honorary women's service group and the Treasurer of the Panhelenic Council. Also, I was very involved with my sorority, with the Honors Business Association, and with a number of other groups.

Q: After you graduated, where did you go to work?

A: I went to work at Pricewaterhouse Coopers after taking a very long summer off and traveling. I started there in September of 1995 with a group called Corporate Finance Recovery and Disputes. This is a consulting group that works primarily in two camps, the first being the bankruptcy and restructuring work, which included turn around and the second being litigation support (i.e. calculating damages for big litigation cases) or any other type of dispute resolution.

Q: Where did you spend your time while working in consulting?

A: I was based in Dallas. I was in bankruptcy and litigation for most of the time I was there. I also did do a couple months in New York. In my last year, my third year at Pricewaterhouse Coopers and during the Asian financial crisis, I spent four months working in Bangkok and then another couple of months working in Columbia.

Q: With all of this experience and things going well, how did you decide to go back to business school?

A: Actually, it was very tough decision because I loved my job — I loved consulting. I had established myself at Pricewaterhouse Coopers. I had good support and networking. I felt that this would be my one chance to do something totally different and that I needed to go in order to have myself be taken seriously outside of Pricewaterhouse Coopers. I also knew that I had a passion to work in Latin America and that, through Pricewaterhouse Coopers, it wasn't an immediate opportunity. I did not want to move to Latin America and be an auditor. I was really curious to learn and study more and be trained to work in Latin American. That was another big reason.

Q: To that end, when did you take your GMAT? Did you take any review courses?

A: No I did not. I actually took my GMAT right after I finished undergrad. I heard that was the thing to do, to take it while you were still "in the study mode." I did not take any review classes but I studied for about a week. I am convinced that this is the way to do it. I sat down for one week with two books... with the Princeton Review book, which I read and big parts of it I just kind of skimmed because I am not a believer in the tricks that it may condone. I do think it does have great tips for grammar and it is a good review. I also sat down with the book that was actually published by the ETS with actual old GMAT's in it. I just worked GMAT after GMAT until I was happy with my score. I then actually ended up exceeding that by quite a good margin.

Q: What schools did you end up applying to and how did you pick them?

A: I ended up applying to Wharton and University of Chicago. The way I picked those was on my passion for Latin American and general international studies. I was really surprised when I started looking at schools at how few of the top ten have a really strong focus in international matters. I could be wrong or be judging too harshly, but it seems like at the schools that did have international and global type programs or majors, I would be spending 2 years sitting in a classroom talking about international issues, but at the end I would not be any more prepared as an individual to actually walk into a board room in Buenos Aires and conduct the meeting with confidence and have all the background knowledge I needed. The only program that seemed to meet this criterion was the one at Wharton, which is called the Joseph H. Lauder Institute of Management and International Studies. It is set up as a dual degree to train people both culturally, linguistically, politically, and economically to be fully versed in international business along side their Wharton MBA experience.

Q: Does that take additional time?

A: I started four months early. It is a very heavy course load. I take on average two additional classes every semester. I would not trade it for the world. The University of Chicago had a similar program but it takes 3 years. In order to graduate in 2 years, I could get what is called an international MBA, an IMBA, at Chicago. The program is about 10 years younger and it did not seem quite as well developed. I ended up getting in both schools and it was a clear choice to go to Wharton. I found out later that

Chicago's program is modeled after Wharton.

Q: Did you feel that the timing of your application was important?

A: People always say that the earlier you get it in, the better. It made a significant difference for me because I moved to Bangkok on three days notice. It definitely made a difference to me. If I had not done them by then, I would not have been able to do it.

Q: On your application, what did you try to emphasize?

A: I know that ninety percent of the people that apply to these schools could tell a similar story to mine — of how they had this great job, were so successful, were promoted. I wanted my application to come to life in a way that would show not only that I was sincere but also reveal what I would bring to a school and ultimately an employer after school. I think Wharton is well recognized in that it is a business as much as it is a school. To a certain extent it is in the business of students. I had to sell myself in that way. I tried to really focus on specific experiences that I had at work and specific types of challenges and how I overcame them. I tried to bring to life also some of the leadership roles I had as an undergrad and how that related to my business experience and how I hoped it would relate to my personal and professional development in the future.

Q: You definitely had a clear picture that you were selling to them.

A: Yes. I think back about the times that I had read applications for organization and resumes for Pricewaterhouse Coopers, etc. and they all just tell a really similar story. They are all very positive. They are all very shallow and boring. They have some compelling things on them, but you see ten or a hundred and they just start to fade together. I did not want to throw the "I want to be an investment banker; I was born to be an investment banker and that is why I need to go to Wharton." First of all, it was not true; second of all, I think a lot of people write that and it just doesn't tell much about a person. I tried to explain what it was about me that made Wharton a perfect fit for me. I think the actual key was that I was not making that up. I was sold that Wharton was a match for me largely because of the Lauder program. It was an easy story to write because it was very sincere.

I actually had MIT tell me point blank that their acceptance rate is very important to them. So if you don't sell them on the fact that you want to go to MIT, your chances of being admitted are actually much, much lower. That is a pretty key point.

Q: Tell my about your letters of recommendations. Who did you choose and why?

A: I chose two people that I had worked with extensively. I chose people that I trusted because I was very secretive about the fact that I was applying to school but I wanted to make sure that they were people who could write letters that came to life. I did not want someone with the traditional "Erica has been a star performer. Erica was promoted early, etc." Those are all great things, but there are a lot of people out there who have the same qualities. I wanted someone who could write a letter of "I worked side by side with Erica in a client room for 6 months and we had some really trying times but she really came through for me in A, B, and C way on X, Y and Z occasions." I wanted a letter that came to life and that was more than just a favor or a generic letter.

Q: Did you have any advisement during your application from colleagues or ex-professors or people that were in business school at the time or were you doing it by yourself?

A: I did it almost entirely by myself. I did have one person who was actually one of the people who wrote my recommendation and served as a mentor for me throughout my time at Pricewaterhouse Coopers. He was a valuable input in the whole process because I asked him when I was finished to review my application for me. He gave it back to me a few days later and said

I don't think you need to go to business school this year. I don't think you are ready because you have not convinced me in these essays. You haven't sold me on it and, if you can't sell me, you can't sell the admissions committee. That was the best thing he could have done for me because he was right. It is a really hard thing to convert what is inside to actually sell it to someone. It was very helpful to get that very harsh opinion right before it actually went out.

Q: Did you wait a year?

A: No, I didn't. I went back and re-wrote and sold it a little bit more. That was his intent. It is not so much what you have done, it is how well you sell it, sadly enough.

Q: Did you have time to do any extracurriculars while you were working?

A: I did some. Not as many as I would have liked — which did not occur to me until I was actually filling out the applications and realized that I became very worked focused. I did have some. I was very involved with my church. I tried to have some sort of a social life when I wasn't working. I did travel a lot and I did work a lot. Within work, I found a lot of extracurriculars in that I wasn't doing pure client work all the time. I made a real point of being involved in recruiting, training, and lunches, happy hours and all that development kind of stuff. A lot of the non-chargeable stuff that is not required but I think is good experience.

Q: Did you have interviews at both schools?

A: I did Chicago on-site in Chicago and I did my Wharton interview in Dallas and my Lauder interview at work.

Q: You had separate interviews?

A: Yes, Lauder has actually a whole separate application process.

Q: Did you try to further unify your ideas from your application or did you try to present a new side of yourself in your interviews?

A: An interview is so short that there was no way I could capture what was in my applications. It seemed liked it was more a reality check to make sure that I could tie my shoes and not trip over both feet. It was much more conversational.

Q: Just allowing you to get to know the school and the school to get to know you?

A: Exactly. There were some questions and some were hard (i.e. give me an example of leadership or challenge you faced in work and how you overcame it). It is certainly much shorter and more painless experience than the application process.

Q: Did you prep for your interviews at all?

A: No. I probably reviewed my application and my resume. It always helps to have those antidotes and stories on the top of your head before walking in because it is so easy to go blank.

Q: Tell me what you are going to do this summer for your internship?

A: This summer I will be interning with Mercer Management Consulting. I will be based in Washington, DC but working most likely in Rio or Mexico.

Q: If you were to give additional advice to someone with a similar background to yourself applying to business school, is there anything you would like to add?

A: To definitely go. You cannot put a price on the experience of an MBA. Not only on the education, but the general life experience is absolutely fabulous. A big part of that for me at least has been the Lauder program and the travel that is required. I have been to Latin America seven times this year, some times through

145

Lauder which requires students to spend the summer in your region of specialization and other times through Wharton. It is just an amazing experience. One you just cannot do in any other way or any other time of your life.

INTERVIEW: HENRY TUNG
Kellogg Graduate School of Management

Q: Tell me your name and your age.

A: My name is Henry Tung and my age is 40.

Q: I know that you have an extensive education history prior to business school, if you could tell me a little bit about that.

A: I want to undergraduate at Stanford from 1977 - 1981. I was a Human Biology major and during that time, I did a bit of research work in laboratories at the Stanford Medical Center, both in oncology and urology. After that I went to medical school at University of California in San Diego. I initially was interested in surgery, but later switched to anesthesia for residency. UCSD happen to have one of the top anesthesia programs in the country. So it worked out real well.

Q: So you stayed there and did your residency?

A: Yes, so I stayed there and did an anesthesiology residency, finishing in 1989. Afterwards I looked at a few jobs around the country. I really did not search that hard. I ended up going to a job in Dayton, OH because I grew had grown up in Ohio. I thought that it was time to go back. It was a great job. A very good private practice. Then a job became available in San Diego with a very well known prestigious group. They were very progressive in terms of their business practices, so that I was attracted to going back to San Diego. I had a lot of professional contacts there. I started in spring 1991 and quickly got into the business aspect of the medical group. It takes two years before you become a full partner. After you are a full partner, you are eligible to be on the Board, and I was elected on the Board the first year I was eligible. I spent some time up to about 1997 on the Board of Directors there and got exposed a lot to the business aspect of health care. Not only about managing the group, which included personal issues and operational issues, but also about outside ventures. They owned outpatient surgical centers. They were one of the first groups or entities to develop that concept back in the early 1970's. We owned the largest chain of outpatient surgical centers in San Diego, which were quite profitable. Eventually, they sold it to a publicly traded company. So I was exposed to a lot of business issues there.

Q: So this peaked your interest in business.

A: Right, we had an MSO, which is a Management Services Organization that we created and spun off from our internal management group and they started managing anesthesia groups around the Western United States. They did the consulting and things like that. I was not directly involved, but I was involved by being a Board member of the parent company. I was involved in a lot of those business decisions. During this time I took some basic finance classes and an eight-month long, one weekend a month, mini-MBA. After you finish it, you can go on to spend one more year in an executive program and get your MBA. It basically taught you the basics of business as it pertained to health care, finance, marketing, etc. I really enjoyed that. It sort of was a test to see if I enjoyed that type of thinking and that type of material. I found that I did. I had a lot of interest in it and I began to see more and more how medicine would be impacted much more by those issues than it would be by the medical or research issues that go on. There really has been a shift in medicine since I was in medical school. It used to be that medicine was dominated by the academic university medical centers. That was were all the research was coming out of. By the time I finished residency that was not true anymore. A lot of the innovation was coming from industry.

I began to realize that private industry was where healthcare and medicine were going towards and I was interested in being involved with that. I was also a little frustrated that, though my group was considered the most progressive one in San Diego, it still was miles behind regular business. The attitude that most doctors have is that their real value is by taking care of patients, not managing the business side. That is what we as doctors get paid for, so why should a person who is doing this other non-clinical stuff get paid much money. After a while, I got tired of butting my head up against the wall. So I started thinking about completing my MBA.

Q: You had a year more of the executive program?

A: Yes, but I thought if I was going to bother to get a MBA, I might as well do it right. As a physician, the only thing you can do with that type of degree is educate yourself for your interest because it does not carry that much weight in terms of the people in the medical community. They don't respect you all that much for your knowledge, because they know you as a doctor first, so it is hard for them to make that transition of what roll you play. If you go outside that community, they look at you and say, okay you are doctor, but you got this MBA at this state school program. It is no big deal. Serious companies, like large corporations, consulting firms, etc. don't pay any attention to those types of MBA's. I did not know exactly want I wanted to do, but I knew I wanted options and I wanted options to pursue business at a higher level. I did not want to stay in the local community and apply my MBA knowledge to a group practice. That is why I decided to apply to a top business school and why I decided to do it full time.

Q: So how did you pick the schools that you applied to?

A: I applied to three schools: Harvard, Stanford and Kellogg. I thought about applying to Michigan, but after looking at is closer, I was not attracted to it. I thought about Wharton, but their admissions office is so swamped, they never sent me an application. I thought that three was enough.

Q: Did you choose those by the personality of the school or by reputation?

A: Mostly by reputation, partly by familiarity, partly with geography issues. I knew that Kellogg was always ranked in the top three and it was in the Midwest, which was close to my wife's family and my family. I wanted my wife to have a support system.

Q: So, when did you take the GMAT?

A: I took it right before I had to, right at the deadline.

Q: Did you take any review courses?

A: No, I didn't take Kaplan or anything like that. I did buy a couple of books just to bone up on some of the basic math and verbal stuff and I found that it was quite easy to use the practice books, which take questions that they said were real ones from the past tests. I took them and did fairly well on them. I took the GMAT and did fairly well. I did not knock it out. I ended up with a decent score, which was about the average for what you needed to get for these top schools. It turned out ok. I did not take a review course. It was not so much the money for me. It was the time commitment to go to these other classes. I didn't feel that it was necessary. I hadn't taken a math class since 1977, 20 years before. Math is one of those things were you can review it a little and you pick it up. I was pretty good in math when I was younger.

Q: Tell me a little more about your application. With your background, you have a lot to say in a small space, how did you choose what you wanted to emphasize?

A: I emphasized my experiences that led to the decision to go back to school, and showed that they were not spurious reasons and that I wasn't a dissatisfied physician. There are a lot of doctors that are just unhappy and they think that they get a business degree, they are going to change the world or at least be able to fight back.

Q: What were you trying to project on your applications?

A: I was trying to project the fact that I had leadership roles and business roles. Also, I discussed my work on a project the year before I applied for business school. I was working on this little project. It was an information system for anesthesia groups. It started as an interest to help my group out and I thought there would be some market demand for this. I met with the COO of the Cardiac Monitoring Company because I was interested in some of their technology. When I was telling him why I was interested, he got so enamored with my idea, he left his job, joined me and we wrote a business plan and pitched it to a bunch of venture capital firms. We did not get funding, but we talked to some of the top firms and they liked our idea, but part of the problem was that the market was too small for what we were doing. It was a very good experience and I learned a lot in terms of how the world worked from an entrepreneur's point of view. I thought that was rather exciting.

Q: If that company had flown, you probably would not have had time to go to school.

A: Exactly. I would not have gone back to business school. As for my applications, I tried to emphasize the positive reasons as to why I wanted to go to business school, to justify it with my previous experiences and try to get across the fact that I was interested in taking a leadership role in the healthcare business. I thought that I could add some value given my experiences in health care. I think part of it was the fact that I had spent some time within health care in significant business and leadership roles. A lot of people who make that transition have not really had that type of experience and so they don't really bring as much to the table. Those were the type of ideas that I tried to get across in my application.

Q: Tell me about your letters of recommendation. Who did you choose to write them?

A: The person that joined me in our quest to get some capital funding. I chose him. One because he was a business person. I chose two doctors and two business people. One was a venture capitalist that I had gotten to know. I did some consulting work for him, which consisted of some due diligence evaluations of medical device companies. He had seen my work and gotten to know me. Obviously, my partner in the entrepreneurial effort got to know me very well and how I think. Both of them had reasonable standing in business. One was a COO and owned venture capital fund. I also got two of my medical partners who both have MBA's. They did the executive MBA route. They understood business and they understand about medicine and they gave me a recommendation based on my work in that group and they evaluated how I dealt with that group, my leadership roles, etc.

Q: What about your interviews?

A: I only interviewed at Kellogg. It was an alumni interview. It was in San Diego not at Kellogg.

Q: Do you think there is a difference between choosing an alumni interview versus coming to the home school?

A: I think going to the home school is helpful just for your own benefit. In terms of getting in, I wouldn't know, simply because I did the alumni route and I got in. I didn't interview at Harvard or Stanford. I did not get accepted at either of those schools. In terms of my grades and performance in business school, I think I was perfectly qualified to go to any of the top schools. In terms of getting in, a lot of it is fairly arbitrary in certain schools. Stanford just has so many applicants. Different schools also have different personalities in terms of what type of people they look for. Stanford attracts the entrepreneurial type and high-tech type. I wasn't so much high-tech. I had some entrepreneurial stuff, although that wasn't my interest in the future. It is hard to know exactly why anybody turns you down. A lot of people who are very qualified to get into business schools will get turned down by any given business school simply for whatever reasons. The lesson there is regardless of how qualified you are, you have to apply to more than one school, just because there is decent chance that you won't get accepted to any given school for whatever reason.

Even if you are grades are fine, your GMAT scores are fine and you have an excellent track record, it doesn't always guarantee that they are going to take you.

Q: As far as your interview, was there anything specific or was it a "get to know you" interview?

A: A lot of it was a "get to know you" interview. I can't recall the questions specifically except for the fact that the questions were fairly open-ended and were designed to look at things like motivation, character, etc.

Q: Something that they couldn't really get off your application.

A: Exactly. It was just the eyeball test. How you carry yourself. All these schools are trying to educate the leaders of business tomorrow. Someone could be very good at writing an essay and could have very good scores, but the moment they walk into a room, you can get a sense by the way they carry themselves, the way they dress, and the way they speak if they are articulate or not and whether or not whether this person is going to make it.

Q: Did you prepare for your interview?

A: No, not at all. I think that part of the reason I got into Kellogg is simply because I am reasonably articulate and I tell a fairly good story. That is what you have to have when you go into these interviews. You have to have a good story. You have to have a compelling reason why you would be a success, why they should accept you. Not just because you want to go and you've got good grades. For the top schools, you need to give them a compelling story. If you read a bibliography of this person, would it be interesting or would you throw the book away after going past two chapters?

Q: After you interviewed, did you update your application with additional information, or did you feel good about what you had?

A: I didn't update it. I felt pretty good about it. I just sent the appropriate thank you letters.

Q: What did you do for your summer internship after your first year of business school?

A: I spent it with McKinsey & Company, a management consulting firm. I was in LA and I did a health care project.

Q: What type of health care arena? Pharmaceuticals?

A: Pharmaceutical growth study.

Q: Are you going back?

A: I am going back to McKinsey but I am going to their NJ office. Their provider practice is in LA and their pharmaceutical/medical device practice is in NJ.

Q: Is there any additional advice that you would give to an applicant with a similar background to yourself?

A: I would say the biggest and most important thing is to do his or her homework. By that I mean, (1) really know why they want to do business school, and (2) get an understanding of what their options are afterwards. They are making a major career change, they should know very well why they are making that career change. I did not know as much as I probably should have, but it turned out okay. Like doing a marketing study, before you launch anything major, you want to know what the market is out there. You want to know what are the possible results and what the probability of achieving them. You wouldn't go off and develop a product if you knew that only 100 people in the world wanted it. That is what you are doing, if you are someone in a specialized situation like a physician and you are going to go to business school, you have to think about what value you add and who is going to want you after business school. If it is just for your own edification, it is not worth it to go the route I am going, simply because it is a lot of money to pay for the school and a lot of lost income.

Q: A huge opportunity cost.

A: It is a huge opportunity cost. For those people, they should do some night school at some local business college. You learn the basic stuff that you will need for whatever you are going to do in your own practice that way. For people who want to make this major commitment, they should sort of find out what is out there. The best way to do that is to talk with people like myself, people who have been in that situation and have gone through the process. You can't really learn by talking to the companies. They really don't know. Even up to this point, McKinsey has a hard time articulating why they hire physicians. They understand that it makes sense in a healthcare practice to hire M.D.'s, but I have asked the top partners in McKinsey in the healthcare practice as to why exactly are they doing it and what is the value added. They don't articulate a very good answer, at least not in my mind.

Q: So talk to somebody that knows.

A: Talk to someone who went through it and had to make the decision and had to do the homework and research. I would be fine for someone talking about industry and consulting. I couldn't tell you as much about investment banking because I did not really investigate that route. There are physicians that went into investment banking. They tend to be a little bit younger than me and not as experienced. I think that is the best way to go about it. If you are going to make a commitment, you should do some homework.

INTERVIEW: BECCA HOFFER
Harvard Business School

Q: Can you tell me your name and your age?

A: Becca Hoffer, and I am 26.

Q: Tell me a little bit about your education prior to business school?

A: I went to a public high school in Beaumont, Texas and then went to the University of Texas. When I got there, I knew I was a business person. I have always been. I have a math mind. I couldn't decide between accounting and finance. After taking a couple of classes and talking to people about their jobs I realized that I needed to be a talker. I couldn't sit behind a desk and crunch numbers all day. I was not going to be an accountant. Finance was it from there on out. I did a semester abroad my junior year in Switzerland at an international business school. It was an American school and everything was taught in English. I chose Switzerland because in my head I thought it was a neutral country and that everyone would speak English over there. I got there and was in a small town, a very small school. I went to Franklin College in Lugano, Switzerland, a school of 200 people, only about 30 of whom were from the U.S. It was a small town on the southern tip of Switzerland close to Italy and absolutely no one spoke English and everyone spoke Italian. It was my first encounter with lots of different cultures and I was impressed because the students could speak so many different languages.

I was a finance major the entire time I was at the University of Texas. I was also very involved in extracurricular activities, most of which centered on my sorority. I had leadership roles with my sorority from the day I started: I was the Pledge Class President and then became Assistant Pledge Trainer the next year, and was Rush Captain my Junior year. I did lots of things at school to put on my resume. The one thing that I was actually interested in was the Academic Standards Committee, which worked on cutting down the student population and on programs for people that didn't get in immediately and had to go through a summer school program prior to admission.

Q: After you graduated, where did you go to work?

A: I worked for the Sanwa Japanese Bank in Dallas for a year and a half. I actually spend my entire senior year of college interviewing. My first semester senior year, I had no idea what I wanted to do. I was going to everything. The second semester, I narrowed it down to banking. I had offers from several domestic banks and then Sanwa Bank. I think it was the largest bank asset-wise in the world at the time. I think I went with them because one, I thought, since they were Japanese, they were going to run the world and they would teach me how to do it; and, two, I was interested in the international aspect.

Q: What did you do for them?

A: I was a credit analyst. I think my title was Banking Associate. We worked with Fortune 100 and Fortune 500 companies. It was a really small branch in Dallas. There were only about twenty of us in the bank and half of them were on the operations side. There were ten of us on the marketing side consisting of six young managers and four credit analysts. The three or four top people in the bank were Japanese. The top managers would be sent over from Japan for about 3 or 4 years at a time to some branch in the U.S. Because of the language barrier, it was difficult to communicate with some of them.

Q: Did that give you more responsibility?

A: Definitely. The way that they worked was really interesting. We didn't lend to anyone that was a big credit risk. The application there was kind of a nightmare. What would happen was we would find a firm or company that we wanted to lend to. I would do everything from a history of the company to all sorts of financial analysis, and come up with a 20 - 30 page application. This would then be sent to Tokyo for approval. Nothing got approved in our office, which is not the way American banks work. Another thing that was interesting was that the Japanese would not lend on cash flow. They lent on assets, which is not the American way of doing it either. We would do this whole application, send it to Tokyo and then go through a Q&A process over the fax machine for weeks. Mostly we were part of syndicated deals where the agent would be a NationsBank or Bank of America and they would do a billion dollar loan and we would take 15 or 20 million out of that.

The interesting part about working for the Japanese was that, business wise, I felt like they were really inefficient. The Japanese men would stay there from 9:00 am to 1:00 am getting work done that you could have gotten done from 8:00 am - 4:00 pm. Not technologically advanced at all, which shocked me. They got computers the day before I started. They didn't use them, didn't want to use them, and would hand us forms to fill out in pencil that they did not want you to do on the computer. You had to fill them out by hand. The next day they would give you some revised form that would be exactly the same information just in a different order and you would have to fill out by hand again.

The cultural differences were amazing. The big one, and the one that made me leave, was the fact that females were not promoted. There were only two of us in the office and we were the only single people. I think they thought we were unstable girls. After my friend there had gotten passed over for a promotion several times, I decided it was time to look for a new job. This was also a company that for my friends who were in their lower 30's were already as high as they could go. There was nowhere else to move. The Japanese were never going to let an American run the bank.

Q: After leaving the bank what did you do?

A: I got really interested in litigation consulting. I started interviewing at different small firms and then finally got to Pricewaterhouse Coopers and had just wonderful interviews there with a partner who explained the entire practice to me. I think at the time it was called "dispute analysis" and corporate recovery was the name of the group. I started out there and did strictly litigation consulting for about the first 6 - 8 months. Then I switched over to the bankruptcy side, which is the work that I definitely loved the most, but I am not sure that I could take the lifestyle for the rest of my life. It was the typical consulting lifestyle of being on the road the entire year. I worked in New York, Columbus, and Miami, FL. I worked on tons of different industries. I worked on the last PanAm bankruptcy, which was one of my favorite jobs. We did a big job in NY at a telecommunications company.

Q: It gave you a good variety of experiences?

A: Definitely. I started toward the end, probably by last 6 - 8 months there, to realize that I really liked doing retail turnarounds. My family has a retail store in Texas. I have grown up with it. It was part of my language. I understood it from day one, unlike the oil and gas industry, which is a completely foreign to me. My last six weeks there I worked with several arts and crafts retailers, which were kind of interesting. I think that was the fad- that they all go bankrupt in about 6 months. I worked on one for a long time. It was probably the only company that I took from 2 months before bankruptcy all the way out of bankruptcy. I wrote my first business plan and from then on out, I thought that was what I loved to do. I became the business plan gooroo of our group and probably wrote 4 or 5 of them until I left, all related to retail.

Q: How did you make your decision to go back to business school?

A: I think business school was in my head from the day I decided I was going to be a business major.

Q: As an undergrad?

A: Yes. I always knew that I needed to go back. I don't know if it was through my parents or just from talking to people at work,

I almost felt like that having a MBA these days was like have an undergrad when they were young. It is a necessity to move up. With Pricewaterhouse Coopers you don't need one. You had to have some other certification to become a manager, but it could have been anything from a CPA to a CFE to a CFA. Any of the different letters you could have behind you name. I really had always thought I was going to go to back to school, but when I applied I loved my job. When I was applying, I guess I was going to be 3 years out. My thought process was that I was going to apply to a few really good schools, knowing that there is a huge chance that I won't get into any of them. If I didn't get in, it would not be a big deal, because I really liked my job and at least I would have the experience of applying and I could apply again next year.

Q: When did you take the GMAT?

A: I took the GMAT in January 1996. I had always heard that studying for the GMAT and taking the GMAT was a lot easier when you were still in the study mode. Actually, when I started studying for it, I wish that you could have taken the GMAT when you were in high school. So much of it is stuff that you have not seen since tenth grade.

Q: Did you take any review courses for it?

A: I took the Princeton Review. I would tell anyone in the world to take a review course. I definitely think that you need one, not that it helps you so much, but I feel like you are at a disadvantage if you don't take it. Almost everyone is taking it. It definitely gives you extra little tips that are going to make you do problems faster, find the right answer without knowing exactly what the question is asking and so you would be kind of behind without taking it. As much as some of these schools tell you that they don't look at the GMAT, I definitely think it is way to weed people out quickly.

Q: How long did you study for?

A: Probably 2 months. Then I had a couple of weeks before the test to study on my own and do practice tests. I think I bought a book before I took the Princeton Review but I didn't open it until I started going there. Classes really make you stick to a schedule. You knew that every week you were going to have to go to the course, whether you wanted to or not. You were paying for it so you were going to go.

Q: Was that hard to do because you were working?

A: I took it when I was at Sanwa in banking. I think at Pricewaterhouse Coopers, a consulting firm or a banking firm it would be much harder. I think you would have to tell somebody that you are taking the course and you are going to need certain nights off.

Q: What schools did you apply to and how did you pick them?

A: I applied to Kellogg, Harvard and Stanford. I also applied to Columbia. To be honest, the only reason I didn't apply to Wharton was because I didn't want to live in Philly. I decided that if I was going to go back to school, and if I made the first cut to get into a great school, I was also going to go to a great school in a great city. That is what I did. I started pretty early trying to find people who had gone to all those schools. I visited as many as I could. I had been to Stanford when I was looking at undergrad. I went to see Kellogg and did the Chicago tour. I was attending a family function in Boston and I went to both MIT and Harvard. This was probably 2 years before I even applied, and I tried to talk to someone at the schools to find out what they were looking for, what I could do to stand out, and all the basic questions that everyone is wondering when they are applying. Harvard would not even let me in the door. They weren't going to talk to me, there was no one there I could meet with. I could walk around by myself if I wanted to. MIT was completely different story. Not only did they let me make an appointment, but ended up sitting down with one of the 5 people on the entrance committee. I sat down with this guy for probably two hours and he gave me some really good advice. He warned me about the new e-mail application. As much as you might think that it is a great way to go and that the school might like it because it is electronic and new age, no one will admit this but a lot of your application is presentation. The school is going to print it out to read it and, when you print out something online, it never comes out the way you would want it to look. He said that really makes a difference, even though it shouldn't. The other thing that he told me is that if there is ever an optional essay, it is really not optional. Never skip a chance to tell these people something about you.

Q: Tell me about your applications? What did you try to emphasize?

A: One of my good friend's sister went to Harvard and she was probably the person that I spoke to the most and I am actually convinced now that maybe that is the reason that I got in there. My advice would be to talk to as many people as you can from the schools that you want to go to. Everyone is looking for something different. Kellogg wants team people. Harvard wants leaders. I talked to a girl from Harvard who said that you should pick out 5 points about your life that you want every school to know about. Then when you are writing, you might want to do just one application at a time and you might not want to start with the one school that you want to go to the most. I started with Columbia since it was at the bottom of my list and started writing. You do start to get confused when you are in the middle of all these essays. I think Columbia only had 5 essays but Kellogg's and Harvard's application are pretty similarly in that they are both small essays but lots of them. I think Kellogg had 8 and Harvard had 6. They are not as long as the other schools but just a lot more. When you start writing, you get confused about what topics you have written about for which school. I definitely wanted to have work experiences in there and made sure that I brought up Sanwa even though it wasn't my most recent experience, just making sure that it was there somewhere. There were interesting parts to my Pricewaterhouse Coopers job and bankruptcy consulting that stuck out from other types of consulting- because I felt that everyone that was applying was either going to be a consultant or an investment banker. I talked about writing business plans. I guess the questions were pretty specific. Several schools ask you about your greatest accomplishments. I went back and forth on whether to include valedictorian in high school. Some people would say that since that experience was too long ago and no one cares what you did in high school and other people would say well if that is still one of your greatest accomplishments, it was kind of neat that you did it. I literally had a list of the 5 things that I wanted to make sure that every school knew about me and if I didn't fit in to anything they asked, then it got thrown into the optional essay. I think that every place I had applied except for Stanford had an optional essay. Stanford's essays were definitely the hardest. I think there are always two essays and they are wide open and could be really long, like 6 or 7 pages. It leaves you to write whatever you want. Fortunately or unfortunately that was the last one I did and I did a lot of cutting and pasting. For most of the applications you can't do that as much as you would think. At first I thought, I just have to write 5 or 6 essays and then I can send them to a lot of different schools. But unfortunately Kellogg and Harvard wanted something in 2 paragraphs and Stanford wanted it in 4 pages, so you just really couldn't do that. It was an interesting process. You really learn a lot about yourself. I was learning much more why I wanted to go back to school than I had even thought about before I started the application process. I think there are a lot of people that think they want to go back and then stop before they ever finish it because of the work. I started in August and sent all my applications out the day before Christmas. I thought that I was going to get something out the first round and then it got to be November and I said that there was no way that any of these could go out.

Q: How did you pick the people who wrote you letters of recommendation? Who were they?

A: I asked two managers from Pricewaterhouse Coopers and a manager from Sanwa. You hear so many different things about how to choose. One is that you don't want to use all business people. You should have someone from the outside world. Two is that you definitely want it to be someone who knows you. I would strongly emphasize this. They really have a lot to fill out and they have to really want to do this for you to do it well. You spend a lot of time wondering if you should ask the highest up person you know and should you have a partner that went to Kellogg or Wharton fill this out for you. If that partner has never worked with you before and if that partner doesn't know you, you have a much better shot of getting in with a letter from Joe Blow that sits next to you and has worked with you for the last year and a half.

Q: You said that you had been investigating the schools for a long period of time. Did you have any additional advisors or alumni that you felt were helpful to talk to? How did you approach getting information?

A: Not necessarily from alumni. I guess just from being on campus. Columbia was the one school that I didn't feel like I had much information about. I happened to be in NY for a wedding and visited Columbia. Columbia has information sessions that you don't have to call in advance for. Once a week they have an information session. I think it was an hour or two. You show up at school and they will tell you about the school. I think it was two students and a facility member. It was very much an eye opener. As much as I heard about Columbia and knew that it was a good school, it was not the place I saw myself. The two students that were there, I don't know if it was the typical student or if this was what they were trying to portray of the school, but they convinced me that this was a commuter school. They were so excited that they could keep their NY apartments and they didn't have to be stuck at school at night and they could just go home back to their normal NY life. Coming from Texas and not having a normal New York life, I was looking for a community and that was not the way they sold the school. This was of course after I had started the application. I thought I would send it in anyway, but hoped to get in somewhere else.

Another thing that I didn't do but would suggest for everyone to do is to go to classes. If you visit these campuses, call the admissions committee and ask if you can go to a class. They are definitely out there for you to go to. Now that I have been in school for a year, you see there are people visiting every single day that will just come sit in class. Of course, now that I am at Harvard and think it is the only place for me, I sit in my interactive classes and think that I could have never been in a traditional lecture environment. I think seeing it kind of puts you at ease and lets you know what you are getting yourself into.

Q: During your work experience, did you have time to do extracurricular activities, be it business related or non-business related or were you working too much?

A: At Pricewaterhouse Coopers, I was definitely working too much. At Sanwa we did a few things in the community as a company. I probably wasn't as active as I should have been. This is probably pitiful to say, but I think a lot of it was resume building and doing things to help me get into business school. This is what everyone had told me I have to do. The one thing that I did while working was actually an interest of mine. I did some work for Race for the Cure in Dallas for breast cancer and it was something that I wanted to do anyway. I think applying to school just pushed me to do it sooner than I would have. But certainly it was worthwhile to do, but it was nothing that I brought up enough in any application. That is something I hope to stay involved in for the rest of my life. I don't know that it played a big part in my applications. I think I might have done one optional essay on it. There were not a whole lot of places that I felt like I should throw it in because I would feel like that they knew I threw it in just because I think that they want to hear it. I didn't end up using it all that much.

Q: You said you had some good stories about your interviews.

A: The interviews were very interesting. Kellogg is, I think, still the only school that makes you interview. I think a lot of the schools are pushing more toward that. I know that at Harvard, in the last two years, 50% of people that they have accepted have had to interview. Harvard and Columbia do interviews on an invitation only basis. I think it is kind of a screener. I decided that if you are right on the edge, let's interview her and see if she can push herself over the edge. I actually ended up thinking that I was going to go abroad for 6 months with work. This was up to the last minute; I was supposed to go to Switzerland for 6 months. I had my bags packed, I had rented out my apartment, everything was done, and I had already applied to these schools. I ended up not going. But the week before I was to leave, I called Columbia and Harvard knowing that they interviewed. I told them I have applied, I was still very interested but I was going abroad for work and asked if there was anything that I could do to make sure that, if I get an interview, I would hear about it or could schedule it in advance. Columbia called me back immediately and said we looked at your application and we can interview you next week in Dallas, not a problem. Harvard called me back and said that it was my responsibility to get my mail when I was out of the country. I asked them that if I went out of the country, would there be someone that I could interview with there. Yes, they told me, we will find you somebody in any country that you want. Completely different responses. I ended up not going abroad, but even before, I think the day after I made the call to Harvard I got the letter that said that they would like to interview me. Kellogg gives you the choice of either coming to the campus or doing it in your hometown. Harvard and Columbia do not do that and they both just sent me letters. Columbia said, here are four people in Dallas, give them a call and make an appointment. Harvard said, here is the lady that will interview you and this is the day you will be interviewing, so call her. I actually did the Kellogg one first. I did that one in December.

Q: Did you do the alumni interview or did you go to the campus?

A: I went to the campus because, of course, I had read every book and every book said that if you have the opportunity to go to campus, you would be letting the school know that you are that much more interested in it. You are there in person to see the school, etc.

After my experience, I would tell everyone, especially if they are from the South, to use alumni. I just had a completely different view and I am not sure if this is what other people think. I never really hit it off with Kellogg person that I interviewed with. I actually interviewed with three women, which I thought was interesting. I always felt that I interviewed better with men. The Kellogg woman was nice and of course I guess I came across as fine and nice. You were in there for 30 minutes and it definitely felt like, after your thirty minutes are up, you are out the door. I never felt like we had a rapport or got along and of course it could just be me looking back on it, trying to come up with some reason why I didn't get in. Even when I left that day, I didn't think that it went very well. With Columbia's interview, I interviewed with the last alumni on the list. She was the only one that could see me within the month. I interviewed with her, she had her computer out in front of her and was typing every word I said the entire time we were talking. I liked her a lot. She actually had a ton to offer. She was extremely bright and gave me a much different perspective on Columbia and got me much more excited about the school that I had been. Probably, for both the Columbia and Harvard "30 minutes interviews", I interviewed for an hour and a half. The Columbia lady was funny. Once we started talking, she said there are certain questions that she was supposed to ask me. Let's just run through those real fast and then we can talk normally. That is when she pulled out the computer and she asked me the questions. They were your basic application questions. She had definitely not seen my application. The questions were- why do you want to go back to school, what are your plans after school, what do you do now, what have you done, where do you want to go to school?

Harvard was very different. Your application certainly helps you answer all these questions, just because you have thought more about yourself in the last 6 months writing these than you have in your entire life put together. Harvard's was probably a good 10 questions and they were situation type questions. Like what you get in consulting interviews but not as technical. It was- tell me about a time that you showed your leadership experience. Tell me about a time that you were in an ethical dilemma. It was kind of like your essays questions, but in a verbal format. She was taking lots of notes too, but it wasn't as quite as disruptive as having the computer. We really hit it off too and she actually told me an interesting statistic. She said that she was interviewing five other people from the Dallas area and that Harvard had told her that 50% of the people that she interviewed would get in. Actually all 5 of us ended up getting in. I don't know if that was just luck of the draw and they gave me someone that said good things about everyone or if they really handpicked these people to do a good job. I think the reason that I said not to go to the school was that, coming from Texas or somewhere from the south, there is an instant rapport with people that are in Texas and they want other people from Texas to be at those schools. People that are from Oklahoma want other people in Oklahoma to get in to Harvard and Kellogg and Stanford. So they are going to do everything they can to get you in that school. It is probably different than being in NY and saying go interview with the local alumni, because that local alumnus has talked to 100 other people whereas the person in Dallas has talked to 5. That was the application process and then you went through the couple months of waiting.

Q: Did you send any additional information?

A: I did send a letter explaining that I was supposed to go abroad and that it was actually a really interesting project.

Q: How did you decide what school was for you?

A: I really feel like you don't have much of a choice. Obviously, I knew that I would be happy at every single one of those schools that I applied to. I felt like Kellogg socially was exactly where I wanted to be. You don't hear about a bad thing about Stanford and Harvard is Harvard. Actually, when I went into my Columbia interview, after I left there, I honestly thought that Harvard might have been the last one on my list. Strictly because of what you hear. Now that I'm there, I feel like none of that is true. The rumors thrown out there are that it is kind of cut throat and you are very independent and not nearly as team oriented as Kellogg and

Stanford, especially Kellogg. I haven't felt that way in the least bit. Just hearing all those things, I knew that it wasn't what I wanted my experience to be like. I remember I found out about all of them in March. On March first, I got my rejection from Kellogg. It was the very first school that I heard from and I thought it was the school that I would get in to. I thought that was the one. They were my favorite essays. Even though I didn't think the interview went that well, they gave you a sheet of paper right when you went into to interview that gave different statistics than you read in the U.S. News and World Reports, etc. Who was ranked where and what kind of scores you need to have to get in where. They showed me statistics saying that of those with 700 - 800 on the GMAT, 35-40% of those people got into school. That is the highest stats I had heard anywhere. I was thinking 10 or 12% at best at any of these schools. About 1 week after that I got a phone call from Columbia that I had gotten in. They left me a voice mail. Then I remembered it was the commuter school and that I had gone up there and not been that excited. Even though the lady that I interviewed with was great, Columbia was not the place for me. I literately went through 2 or 3 weeks of talking to every single person that I knew about whether it was worth my going to Columbia or if I should just stay with my job another year. I had so many friends that were applying to school just because they wanted to quit their jobs, but that was certainly not my case. I pretty much decided that I was going to apply again. I would go up and see the school again, but, if this were the only place I got into, I would apply again next year. Stanford and Harvard tell you the exact day that you will get them and they are right on. Stanford was mailing theirs March 25th and Harvard was mailing theirs March 26th. I was out of town when Stanford mailed out their letters. I received a very thick envelope from Stanford in the mail and my boyfriend read my rejection from them. The reason why it was so thick is because Stanford sends you a Q&A of frequently asked questions by people that don't get in. One of the questions was, "should I apply again?" and the answer was, "probably not." This was a printout, the same thing obviously went to everyone that applied but I just thought it was very interesting.

Q: Then another envelope came for you that was very good?

A: Yes. That Monday, I was on a job out of town and got a thin envelope from Harvard. It said congratulations at the top. That was the best day. It was frustrating that I was on an out of town project and it was my first day on that project so I was there with people that I didn't know and was calling everyone in the world that night to celebrate over the phone instead of being out somewhere. There was no thought process in deciding what school to go to. I kept thinking back that I thought that they were not very nice when I called and asked questions and then when you get in it is just a complete 180. As soon as you call after you get in, one of their first questions is "have you been admitted" or "are you just calling to ask us questions" and once you say you are an admit, they are the nicest people in the world. I received calls from people on the Student Association asking me if I had any questions about anything.

Q: So, this summer, after your first year, what are you doing for your internship?

A: I am actually sponsored by Pricewaterhouse Coopers. I think there are about six others throughout the country that are sponsored in different schools. The sponsorship is a little bit different. In most cases, the sponsor doesn't want you to go work for the competitor, but they want you to go into industry, gain skills that you can bring back to the firm. Pricewaterhouse Coopers does not think that way. They wanted me to come back for the summer and that was actually part of my deal with them. When I originally signed a deal with them, my thought was that I probably could handle consulting for another 3 years, but I know I don't want to do it for the rest of my life. I just don't see myself having that lifestyle. When I got to school, I was sleeping less in school than I was in consulting. My first semester, I probably averaged 4 hours a night. I realize that I can't go back to the consulting because I can't do this. I have to sleep. Then I started looking into other things to do. We have a CEO on campus every week and every single one of them opens their mouths at the beginning with, "our people are our only competitive advantage these days" — trying to push all these Harvard people into working for their companies. I really started to think about that and I had always been interested in Human Resources (H.R.) but had never thought I could make a living out of it. I liked the recruiting side and all the aspects of H.R. I started looking into it and found out that every single investment bank had summer programs in H.R. It is a really big deal and they are pulling people off the line to do it. So, I started making cold calls. They did not come to campus to recruit for any of this because I don't think that they think there are Harvard people that are interested. I started talking to Pricewaterhouse Coopers about the possibility of doing Human Resource work and got really interesting reactions.

My group now is a global Human Resources group. I am not necessarily in the trenches doing recruiting and staffing and compensation. We're a global H.R. team of about 6 or 7 people that are doing bigger initiatives like cost cutting initiative (how do we find the synergies between Pricewaterhouse and Cooper's, and if we cut our turnover by 1%, we save the company X million dollars.) There is definitely a financial side to H.R. There is also the creative side as well. It has been interesting so far. For me it's definitely been the right choice with much better hours than all of my roommates and all of the people that I have talked to in NY. I am happy. It amazed me that, during my off-campus recruiting search, I could leave a message with the Managing Director of Merrill Lynch saying I was interested in human resources and he would call me back within 5 minutes. You don't even get that response rate with your bosses. This was a random MBA student cold calling and then you throw the name Harvard out. They call you back in five minutes! I think you would get that response with Kellogg, Wharton or Stanford. Certainly one of the best parts of these schools is the networking. You have that for the rest of your life. It gets you in the door, and you have to sell yourself after that, but at least it gets you in the door.

Q: Is there any other advice that you would like to give?

A: My only other advice would be to start early. I really thought it was going to be a much shorter process. I started in August and thought I would have all my applications in by October or November and I was pushing to get them out the door by the end of December. Definitely, all the advice that you hear about applying to one of the first 2 rounds vs. the 3rd round is definitely good advice. You want them to see you first before they have everyone else on their plate to compare you to. Anything you can think of in your life that would kind of make you stand out, throw it in even though it is not all that relevant. I think it's important to talk to the people that go to those schools. I think that if I had talked to more people that went to Kellogg, they could have said this is what they wrote on my application and this is what got them in. Kellogg really didn't give me a reason why I didn't get in and certainly told me to apply again. By talking to someone from Harvard, I was able to write my essays in a Harvard style. I think there is definitely a style that they are looking for. Every single one of my Harvard's essays wasn't just "this is what I have done," but it was "this is what I have learned and will take with me from this experience." That is the kind of stuff that Harvard is looking for.

Kellogg Graduate School of Management

Q: Can you tell me your name and your age?

A: Sara Rudstein and I am 28.

Q: Can you tell me about your education prior to business school?

A: I went to the University of Pennsylvania for undergrad and I graduated with degrees in Theater Arts and English.

Q: While you were an undergrad, what type of activities did you participate in?

A: Mostly activities with the theater. I was going between being a sports writer or working for newspaper or going into theater. I went back and forth for 2 years and then, in my final 2 years, I pretty much settled on theater.

Q: Were you in a number of productions?

A: I mostly directed. I did stage management and some technical theater... some acting, but my focus was directing. My concentration in my theater major was directing. I fell into that really early in school and tried to do as much of that as possible.

Q: So you hadn't planned on a business degree or a career?

A: No, I thought I would graduate and be a director. I was all set to go to New York. I was going direct and this weird set of twists and turns lead into the theater administration.

Q: What happened when you left college after you graduated?

A: Two things actually. I left college and produced and directed a show that went to Edinborough, Scotland. It was a lot of coordinating with the theater over there... coordinating transportation or the technical aspects of a show. It really gave me exposure to the management side of theater and I decided that I really liked it. I found it very interesting. I moved and, through another turn of events, I met somebody in DC with a lot of experience. He said that I should go to a smaller theater town before I went to NY and try to build up my resume and then hit NY. I thought this sounded perfectly reasonable. I moved to DC, which was a great theater town and started looking for jobs wherever I could find them. I thought that I would take a job in one of the offices and then I would network with people and get over to the directing side. I got a job with The Olney Theatre Center for the Arts and worked in the development office. I found that a transition over was much harder than I anticipated. I worked there for a while, but thought that maybe I was too far away from the production side of theater. Then I started stage-managing for them in hopes of going into directing. The strangest thing was that I realized that I missed the overall planning for the theater. I missed the managerial end and administrative part. I knew the type of job I wanted, but it was just a question of waiting for something to open up. Finally a job opened up in the Shakespeare Theatre. It was as a company manager, which is a nice blend between the creative and the artistic. You deal a lot with the artistic company, the cast, the designers and play a supporting roll in helping them with all their administrative needs throughout the process as well as dealing with the administrative duties to go along with that. My boss there, who was managing director, had an MBA. The director of finance had an MBA. The two of them were very adamant that I should go the MBA route rather than the MFA route (Fine Arts & Administration), which the majority of people in theater with graduate degrees have. I thought about that for a really long time and I said an MBA is transferable to anything, and I still want to go back into theater. I figured having an MBA would give me one step up on people with an MFA.

Q: So you made the decision. How did you make it come true?

A: I was thinking about it for a really long time before I finally decided. I thought about it for a few years before I decided to apply. Once I finally made the decision, I knew that I wanted to take on more responsibility. I knew that I could do a lot more than they were giving me. They also recognized that I was an under-grad. I never took a business course. I never even thought twice about business. I wanted to take on all these great projects but I really didn't have the basics to know what I was doing. I talked to people along the way and tried to figure out what I needed to know and try to do it that, but the easiest way for me to ever do this is to go back to school. I just decided I was going to make the commitment. I studied for the GMAT. I kind of thought that it really didn't matter where I got my MBA, so I thought about working at the Shakespeare Theatre and going to the University of Maryland part-time. I don't know how I did it, but I did really well on the GMAT and then I decided to shoot for the stars. Why not apply to these great MBA programs and go back full-time for 2 years.

Q: How did you study for the GMAT? Did you take a course?

A: I took a Kaplan course.

Q: Was that helpful? The structure?

A: Very helpful because it had been so long since I had taken a standardized test. It had been a good 8 or 9 years. I had been thinking about this for a very long time and I had gone out and bought some books to study on my own and they really were not helping. So when I finally made the commitment, I knew that I would have to take a course because I didn't know what I was doing.

Q: How long did you study? How many months?

A: I took the test in November and I took probably 2 - 3 months to study.

Q: Did you study everyday or when you could?

177

A: It would be the type of thing that I would have my books with me and I'd turn to them whenever I had a slow period at work (although nobody knew that I was studying for them). Whenever I had some free time on my own, I studied.

Q: How did you choose the schools that you applied to?

A: I looked at a lot of factors. Entertainment and theater were considerations, and non-profit was a consideration. I basically relied a lot on the Business Week survey and the Business Week book on which schools were strong in the areas I wanted- as well as on their reputations. My brother had just applied to business school the year before and he is one year ahead of me. He went through all these things, so he was a resource also.

Q: How many schools did you end up applying to?

A: Six.

Q: Which ones were they?

A: Kellogg, Olin, Andersen, Yale, Columbia and Maryland. I actually ended up withdrawing half of them. I got into Olin. It was the first one I got into. I visited and loved it. Both Columbia and Maryland wanted to interview me. I decided not to take either one on top of Olin. Most people were surprised that I didn't take Columbia. I knew it was going to be either Kellogg or Olin. It was just a question of whether I could get into Kellogg.

Q: Tell me about your applications. You have a very different background compared to a lot of the MBA students. What did you try to project in your application?

A: The application was the worst process I have ever gone through in my life. Partly because by the time I took the GMAT, it was November and applications were due starting in November or December. I took the GMAT and was just going to apply to Maryland. Then I decided to apply to some others after I found out my GMAT was competitive. Kellogg and Yale were the non-profit schools. Columbia and Andersen were the entertainment schools. I liked Olin because it had the reputation of being a smaller version of Kellogg (also I was a Wash. U undergrad.). Olin had a very good, very positive write-up in Business Week. All of a sudden I had these six applications to do in a month, maybe a month and half. By that point, I was able to tell my boss that I wanted him to write me a recommendation. He was the only one I told. He was incredibly supportive.

Every spare second I had was all about applications. I knew that I had an unusual background so I played it up to the biggest extent I possibly could. I knew that I was a long shot at every single one of these schools except for Maryland. Maryland was my state school so I though that I could get in there. I had absolutely nothing to lose. I took a couple of chances. I made some essays a lot more human — which some schools like and some schools don't. . Fortunately, Kellogg did. I just tried to take as many chances as I could and go out there and project my unusual background. I knew the interview would be key. Actually, Andersen would not let me interview with them because they had an invitation-only policy. All of the other schools I set up interviews with. Columbia was invitation only, but I got an interview there.

Q: You talked briefly about your letters of recommendations. Who did you pick?

A: I had my boss, the Executive Director of the Helen Hayes Awards and who was my mentor from the second I got to DC. Every step along the way, she had been very supportive. She was just a natural for me to ask. My third one was the President of WGMS radio in Washington. She was just someone who I had worked on a cultural alliance with. We worked pretty closely together and we really just hit if off. She is a very enthusiastic person and very supportive of my decision.

Q: During this time, what other extracurricular activities were you involved with?

A: The Helen Hayes Awards for the past 8 years as Assistant to the Director. That was also very seasonal, just throughout April to beginning May.

Q: What are the Helen Hayes Awards?

A: They are Washington's version of the Tony Awards. It is for excellence in Washington Theater. I also volunteered with a home for terminally ill children when they are coming to undergo treatment in NIH. It is a place for them to stay with their families. There is a staff of about 8 and run by a large part of volunteers.

Q: What did you do with them?

A: I was a volunteer resident weekend manager. I would go various weekends and oversee operations. Basically, they had a full time person there during the week there for emergencies, etc. and they gave her weekends off. So then they relied on volunteers to come in. It was wonderful.

Q: How many interviews did you end up going on?

A: Three: Kellogg, Olin and Yale. I thought I needed every ounce of support I could get. I thought that interviews were where I would really sell myself. I'm very comfortable in an interview situation. I just knew that I had to go in there and sell myself because my background is so unusual. I had to go in there with the attitude that this is what I want to do, this is where I want to go and hope that they liked me. Kellogg did.

Q: Do you remember anything about your interviews that impressed you?

A: I really hit it off with my Kellogg interviewer the best and I thought it worked the best. She just re-stepped through my resume. How did you get here and how did it link back to where you are now? This was something I was very comfortable with talking about. The Olin interview wasn't really like an interview.

It was basically, did you have any questions for me. It was by somebody in the office. It was during their preview weekend. They gave me somebody who was exceptionally nice and asked a couple of questions, but they weren't too in depth, stressful or strenuous. It was more for me to get to know the school. Yale was a difficult interview. Unlike Kellogg and Olin, it did not feel like they wanted me to succeed as much. I felt that there was a lot more resistance there. I took calculus and statistics before coming to business school to prepare for what I knew was going to be difficult. For Kellogg and Olin, that was a wonderful thing. Yale was more an argumentative interview.

Q: Did you send anything else in after your interviews or later in the process to the schools?

A: Just follow up thank you notes.

Q: Is there anything else for someone that has a non-traditional background, like yourself, that you feel is important to the application process that you would like pass on?

A: Find schools that are really accepting of the non-traditional students. I think schools are starting to be more accepting of it. I think Kellogg was a trendsetter, because everybody here is more interesting than the next person. Everybody I meet has the most interesting background. I know Olin is really trying hard to do that. Other schools are doing that as well. It is just a question of finding a fit with the school. When I visited here, I knew that this was the place for me. I didn't know if I could get in, but I knew that if I got in, it would be the right decision. I felt that at Olin, too. Even though Columbia was at the time was number six and Olin was sixteen in the ratings that wasn't as important to me as the fit. I think the fit is everything.

Q: What are you planning to do for your summer internship after your first year of business school?

A: It was a really tough decision what to do for an internship. I decided I wanted to do something completely opposite of my background. One, to see if I liked it and two, just because I knew that I couldn't get a good theater internship that would really go in depth in any one theater for the summer. Since I was pretty certain and still am that this is what I want to do, I felt that it really wouldn't do anything for me. I really targeted the areas of both sales and marketing. It was the only aspect of theater that I had no previous experience in. I will be working for Kraft in Sales Strategy.